Anne Bancroft

ZEN

Direct pointing to reality

with 107 illustrations, 15 in colour

Thames and Hudson

ART AND IMAGINATION

© 1979 Anne Bancroft
Reprinted 1993

Printed and bound in Singapore by C.S. Graphics

Contents

墨卷一張紙
畫畫人間事
對面似忘機說
出管妙義名稿
飛溪溅岳出戎
眉頭出真岳歌
華頂河

Han-shan, a lunatic Zen monk of the Tang Dynasty, unrolls the scriptures.

Every religion at its highest tells us that life itself is holy, and that the full experience of the transcendent nature of life is a homecoming. Zen is a Buddhist way of attaining a direct realization of the truth of these statements. Based on the highest teachings of the Buddha, it was taken in the sixth century AD from India to China, where it came to be known as 'direct pointing to the heart of man'. This direct pointing is to the living experience of Reality, to what life is in itself, unmediated by words or ideas. Zen points to a specific state of awareness in which the mystery and beauty of life in this very moment is perceived wholly and directly and with pure objectivity. In the words of one of its teachers, Dogen, 'To learn the way of the Buddha is to learn about oneself. To learn about oneself is to forget oneself. To forget oneself is to be enlightened by everything in the world. To be enlightened by everything is to let fall one's own body and mind.'

Zen is a religious path, but it expresses Reality not in theological explanations but in everyday conversation and advice. On how to act in accordance with Reality, Ummon says:

> When walking just walk,
> When sitting just sit,
> Above all, don't wobble.

And that age-old problem of how to live in the world, and yet find liberation, is dealt with in this fashion: Bokaju was once asked, 'We have to dress and eat every day, and how can we escape from all that?'

The master replied, 'We dress; we eat.'

'I do not understand.'

'If you do not understand, put on your clothes and eat your food.'

The usual conceptual mode of thinking is upset by the apparently unsatisfying advice given in this last statement – the logical mind has nothing to feed on. Intellect and imagination are told to come to a full stop so that eating food and dressing can be experienced as they really are.

Because Zen desires to loose us from the grip of concepts, to shatter the rigid thought-forms in which we seek to possess life, it also makes devastating use of contradiction and paradox. When Joshu, a great Zen master, was asked what he would give when a poverty-stricken man should come to him, he replied, 'What is wanting in him?' When he was asked on another occasion, 'When a man comes to you with nothing, what would you say to him?' his instant reply was, 'Throw it away!' Our intellect may make little of this but our innate sense of being, which is what Zen is trying to awaken, will recognize immediately this man who is presenting 'having nothing' as a personal belonging. Paradox is a well-known means of presenting religious truth. For instance, the nobleman in Christ's parable of the talents (Luke 19:26) says 'Unto every one which hath shall be given; and from him that hath not, even that he hath shall be taken away from him.' Zen, too, uses concrete presentation rather than abstraction. For instance, according to Fudaishi:

> Empty-handed I go and yet the spade is in my hands;
> I walk on foot, and yet I am riding on the back of an ox:
> When I pass over the bridge,
> Lo, the water flows not, but the bridge is flowing.

But if paradox is baffling, it is nothing compared to the Zen denial of opposites, the way it sees the truth by using neither assertion nor negation. Ummon says, 'In Zen there is absolute freedom: sometimes it negates and other times it affirms; it does either way at pleasure.' Zen masters in ancient China used to carry a short stick known as a chu-pi. Pi-mo, a noted master of the tenth century, used to carry a forked chu-pi and whenever a monk came up to him and made a bow, he would put the stick to the neck of the monk and say, 'What devil taught you to be a homeless monk? What devil taught you to walk about? Whether you can say something or whether you can't, just the same you must die under my fork: speak, speak, be quick!'

This 'Speak, speak!' (used by many masters) is again an attempt to awaken the true person. Most of our days are spent responding to the world in the ways we think it expects of us – which brings about the belief that we have a number of characteristics adding up to a 'personality'. But no acquired aspect of ourselves has a chance to respond to that peremptory 'Speak, speak!' Only the real person has a chance of survival there.

In these ways, Zen denies all attempts to rationalize it, make sense of it, or turn it into a philosophy, and it compares man's desire to grasp it intellectually to a finger pointing at the moon – the finger continually being mistaken for the moon itself. It has an amused indifference to the worldly goals of men. The Zen outlook has it that all is equally holy – even straw mats and horse dung – and to distinguish one of life's aspects and make it of more importance than another is to fall into dualistic error rather than reality. A famous Zen poem says:

> The perfect way knows no difficulties
> Except that it refuses to make preferences;
> Only when freed from hate and love
> It reveals itself fully and without disguise;
> A tenth of an inch's difference,
> And heaven and earth are set apart.
> If you wish to see it with your own eyes
> Have no fixed thoughts either for or against it.

The classic instance of such an attitude is the arrival in China of Bodhidharma, a renowned Indian Buddhist of the sixth century, who came to teach Zen and stayed to become China's First Zen Patriarch. On his arrival he was received by the Emperor Wu, a Buddhist convert, who related all that he had done in the way of building temples, translating the scriptures, and converting men and women to monastic life. He asked Bodhidharma what merit this would bring him and was very put out by that uncompromising monk's reply of 'None whatever. A true deed of merit comes straight from the heart and is not concerned with worldly achievements.'

'Then what is this holy religion all about?' asked the Emperor.

'Vast emptiness, and there's nothing holy in it.'

Such an answer is of the same nature as the one given to a novice who made a respectful remark about the Buddha. He was told to rinse his mouth out and never to utter that dirty word again.

To one who practises Zen any such term as 'holy' or 'Buddha' is a trap, implying the reality of such things when in fact they only exist as concepts in the mind. Zen masters, when they met each other, would rock with laughter at the idea that they were supposed to be holy and worthy of reverence and would often caricature each other in portrait form as rotund or absurdly wizened old men, with such titles as 'a bag of rice' or 'a snowflake in a hot oven'. They would delightedly set traps, trying to trick each other into conceptual statements about enlightenment or Buddhism or Nirvana, and burst into laughter when the trap was subtly acknowledged or avoided.

The Zen way of teaching is to demonstrate Reality rather than talk about it, and is always to be taken seriously, although it is never solemn. To see it in its proper teaching capacity we have to overcome our tendency to put everything into words. Words are essential; but the snag is that when we rely too much on words we begin to substitute a world of indirect knowledge – knowledge *about* – for the immediate intense impact of what is actually there before thoughts and words arise. By using the right words for each situation, we can live our lives through without ever experiencing anything directly. The central methods of Zen are aimed at helping a pupil see that the conventional ways in which the world is conceptualized are useful for particular purposes but lack substance; when the concept-world is broken through, the pupil will come to the experience of unmediated Reality – the discovery of the ineffable wonder which is existence itself.

The originator of Zen teaching is believed to have been the Buddha, on an occasion when he was staying at Vulture Park and giving daily discourses to his followers. One morning he arrived to find twelve hundred people seated, waiting for him to speak. He sat in front of them in silence. The time went past but still there was silence. At last, silently, he held up a flower. Nobody understood this gesture except one person, who smiled, having seen that no words could be a substitute for the living flower. The Buddha said, 'Here is the true Way and I transmit it to you.'

In this way he pointed out that the unmediated experience of existence – the here-and-now experience – is a profound mystical insight. The phenomenal world is seen as it is, in its 'isness', without the projection of 'I'.

When Buddhism came to China it brought with it strands of its own cultural background. The Buddha was an Indian prince of the sixth century BC, and Indian religion has always been characterized by the quest to find the One behind the many, the absolute Reality of the universe beyond all opposites. In ordinary life all things and experiences have opposites – life is opposed to death, night to day, pleasure to pain, light to darkness. But in Hindu religion Reality has no opposite, it is non-dual, and man is delivered from suffering and death when he realizes his identity with Reality. In the *Upanishads*, the Hindu scriptures, this Reality was given the name Brahman. Not to realize Brahman, as the essential One manifesting as oneself, is ignorance and suffering; to become aware of it is true enlightenment and transcendent happiness – a happiness which does not fade, because it too has no opposite.

Early Indian Buddhism also looked for the One Reality, but its approach was psychological rather than religious. The Buddha felt that philosophical speculation about Reality was a barrier to the immediate and intimate experience of it, and that this could only be had by letting go of the craving and greed which keeps man bound to the world. Later Indian Buddhism, in the form of the Mahayana school (of which Zen is one of the fruits), returned to some extent to the philosophical tradition, but came to a new understanding of the nature of Reality – an understanding inherent in the Buddha's actual teachings but not attained by early Buddhists. The Mahayana school realized that the concept 'all things are Reality' implicitly opposes 'all things' to Reality and then tries to create a union. Reality and all things are already united, and to *make* a union either in thought or feeling is to give oneself the idea that it does not already exist. In thought they can be separated, but in actuality there is no separation. Nirvana (the state of Reality) *is* Samsara (the state of ordinary life) and to use such a term as the One, or Brahman, or God, is inappropriate.

In our own time this point has been made clear by Father William Johnston, a Jesuit who went to meditate in a Japanese Zen monastery and recorded his impressions in a book, *Christian Zen*. He relates that after sitting in meditation for some time his legs began to ache terribly. The master gave him advice on this and then asked him what practice he was following in his meditation. Johnston replied that he was sitting silently in the presence of God without words or thoughts or images or ideas. The master asked if his God was everywhere, and when he replied yes, asked if he was 'wrapped around in God'. The answer was again yes.

'And you experience this?' asked the master.

'Yes.'

'Very good, very good,' said the master, 'continue this way. Just keep on. And eventually you will find that God will disappear and only Johnston remain.'

Johnston was shocked by this remark because it sounded like a denial of all that he had thought of as sacred. He decided to contradict the master and said, smilingly, 'God will not disappear. But Johnston might well disappear and only God be left.'

'Yes, yes,' the master answered, smiling, 'It's the same thing. That is what I mean.'

So for Mahayana Buddhism, man cannot in actuality be separated from God, the actor cannot be separated from his acting, energy from mass, or life from its manifestations. When we split them one from the other in our thoughts and then believe these thoughts to be the truth, we suffer intellectually, morally and spiritually. But how, then, can we refer to Reality?

In order to speak about it at all, Mahayana termed it Tathata (Suchness), or Thusness, and Sunyata (the Void), considered not as mere emptiness but as dynamic living Voidness, ungraspable and timeless, the true nature of which remains unknown. The Suchness of life is sensed, not thought, and when it is apprehended its Void nature is realized. This state of non-grasping and freedom from craving is both spiritual and psychological.

These were the interwoven developments of Buddhism which came to China in the early centuries AD and which in their turn were deeply influenced by Taoism as taught by Lao-Tzu (sixth century BC) and Chuang-Tzu (third century BC). In Taoism, Reality is termed Tao, a word which has no real translation but which has a more practical, dynamic understanding than Brahman or Sunyata. Tao is life sensed as a flowing movement, a power like the wind or water. It is sometimes termed 'the Way of things' and one who is in accord with it is said to be in a state of Te, or grace. The method of realization is called Wu-wei, or non-assertion, which is very similar to the Buddhist freedom from craving. As in Buddhism, all evil actions and all suffering are thought to stem from man's belief in himself as separate from Tao; from his aggression and ego-assertiveness; and from his incessant desire to possess life, particularly in the fixed forms of concepts and ideas. If man could realize that he is at one with the fullness of life, if he could cease from aggressive ego-assertion and let go of his grasp of his own life, then life or Tao would be able to operate freely within him. His life would be lived not by the dictation of his own ego but by Tao.

The goal of Indian religion was the realization of man's identity with Brahman or Tathata, and of the essential unity underlying the apparent opposition of Reality and appearance, of Nirvana and Samsara; and, for the Chinese, harmony with the Tao was the main object. To Indian religion the attainment of complete realization meant deliverance for man from the round of birth and death as we know them and the passing of his consciousness out of this realm of manifestations. But Chinese religion felt no pressing need to transcend everyday consciousness. Man was at one with Tao here and now, did he but know it, and his usual consciousness of people and things was the working of the Tao. When it first came to China, Mahayana still retained some of the Indian desire to escape from the ordinary world of physical form; but under Taoist influence it lost this feeling completely and became a world-transforming instead of a world-escaping religion.

Thus Zen came into being through the merging of the Hindu–Buddhist understanding, that the essential Reality of life can be discovered through non-attachment to any of its particular forms, and the Taoist discovery that the harmony of life with Tao can be realized by letting go of that life so that it is free to be itself. The traditional Buddhist practice of meditation became the chief method of realization, and the Zen school was named after it. The word Zen is a Japanese rendering of the old Chinese word Ch'an, which in its turn was taken from the Indian word Dhyana, all meaning a meditational way of life in which the present moment is lived with full attention and clear awareness.

In an early sutra, the Buddha taught: 'In what is seen there should be just the seen; in what is heard there should be just the heard; in what is sensed (as smell, taste or touch) there should be just the sensing; in what is thought there should be just the thought.' Many centuries later these words were echoed by Zen masters from both China and Japan, who, when asked for teaching, would give such a reply as: 'When you bring me a cup of tea, do I not accept it? When you make bows to me, do I not return them? When do I ever neglect to give you teaching? If you want to see, see directly into it; when you try to think about it it is altogether missed.'

The aim of Zen training is to attain the state of consciousness which occurs when the individual ego is completely emptied of itself and becomes identified with the infinite Reality of all things. This experience, known by its Japanese name of satori, is 'the state of consciousness in which Noble Wisdom realizes its own inner nature' according to the *Lankavatara Sutra* (which uses the term 'perfected knowledge' for this state). It is an immediate seeing into the nature of things instead of the usual understanding through analysis and logic. In practice it means the unfolding of a new and changed world, a world previously hidden by the many confusions of the dualistically oriented mind. All contradictions are harmonized by the miracle of satori, and the experience is one involving the whole person, not a mere psychological insight or highly charged ecstasy. Satori leads to a total revaluation of the personality, and, perhaps even more important, it opens the mind to a wider and deeper feeling for life, so that even the most trivial incidents and tasks gain new significance. Ever since the development of human consciousness, man seems to have responded to his inner and outer conditions in a conceptual way. The experience of satori upsets this conditioned framework once and for all.

The numinous quality of the experience – in which the *radiance* of the world is revealed as never before – transforms ordinary subject–object duality into a new dimension of being, so that there appears to be an absence of self or 'I' for as long as the experience lasts. This is the state of poverty and emptiness described by the mystics of all religions, and to attain this state of being is to discover the meaning of one's own existence, to find one's true place in the flux of life, to identify oneself with, and to love, everything that exists.

Satori is the pivot of Zen life. It is at once the last and the first step, the goal and the beginning, because to attain satori is to experience the natural state of the mind from which all good actions flow and in which there is an illumined recognition of the harmony of life. The result is to become properly human, relating to other people with an awareness and awakened insight which is free of self-interest. This may take years to reach full growth, which is why it is considered a first step as well as a last, but satori is the stick which sounds the gong and shatters the silence of ignorance. To the one who has experienced this turnabout in his nature, life becomes ever more 'empty and marvellous'.

> *He who holds that nothingness*
> *Is formless, flowers are visions,*
> *Let him enter boldly!*

(An inscription over Lin-chi's door)

There are many descriptions of satori in Zen literature. The sixteenth-century master Han Shan says of the enlightened man that his body and mind are entirely non-existent: they are the same as the absolute Void. Of his own experience, he writes: 'I took a walk. Suddenly I stood still, filled with the realization that I had no body or mind. All I could see was one great illuminating Whole – omnipresent, perfect, lucid and serene. It was like an all-embracing mirror from which the mountains and rivers of the earth were projected. . . . I felt as clear and transparent as though my body and mind did not exist at all.'

Modern western descriptions of satori sound a little more self-conscious, but still have the authentic ring of jubilation. A Canadian housewife records, 'The least expression of weather variation, a soft rain or gentle breeze, touches me as a miracle of unmatched wonder, beauty and goodness. There is nothing to do: just to be is a total act.' And an English schoolteacher says: 'There was a blackbird in the garden, and it was as though there had never been a blackbird before. All my inner turmoil melted away and I felt full of clarity and indescribable peace. I seemed at one with everything around me and saw people with all judgment suspended, so that they seemed perfect in themselves.'

Attachment to the ego, and enslavement by feelings and ideas about it, is the basic cause of man's fears, worries and miseries, taught the Buddha. The Zen methods of liberation are intended to cut through our tangles of desire and repulsion, dreams and longings, fears and angers. Most of all, Zen attacks our reliance on habitual ideas. Over and over again, a Zen master will roar 'Ho!' at a pupil who has asked some question about the teaching, for he sees that the pupil is living from concepts instead of Reality. When a monk earnestly asked Joshu, 'When the body crumbles all to pieces and returns to the dust, there eternally abides one thing. Of this I have been told. But where does this one thing abide?' Joshu replied, 'It is windy again this morning.'

Zen seems to offer nothing to theology. It has no creed or dogma. It does have many scriptures, not only the general Buddhist sutras but also its own discourses and mondo, dialogues between masters and pupils which illustrate methods of instruction. Zen also employs images and symbols and the normal structure of the Buddhist religion. But Reality cannot be bottled up in any definition, and certainly not equated with it, and so the idea that the scriptures will do any more than point the way is firmly resisted, some disciples even being ordered to tear their scriptures to shreds. Zen is not interested in high-flown statements; it wants its pupil to bite his apple and not discuss it.

The training by which the pupil is enabled to let go his hold on his concept-world is applied through four main avenues: zazen (sitting meditation), koans (problems beyond logic), sanzen (private interviews with the master), and ordinary physical work in monastery and gardens – the practice of which brings the others into accord with everyday life.

Strictly speaking, Zen does not believe that any method can awaken the mind to Reality, because this implies a self-conscious attempt to grasp something which is already present, and methods are considered as misleading as 'putting legs on a snake'. On the other hand, the technique of zazen has emerged over the centuries, particularly in Japan, as a successful (many would say necessary) discipline which enables the mind to settle into itself in a way which is relaxed yet attentive, free and yet concentrated.

In zazen, the pupil sits cross-legged in the yogic lotus position and by slow, rhythmic breathing (sometimes counting the breath is used as an aid) he brings his mind to a state which is calm and free from ideas and chatter. In some meditations he simply keeps to this mode of being by allowing thoughts to come in and go out of his head like clouds across the sky, neither holding on to them nor pushing them away. In other meditations he may take up the koan or mondo set him by his master and allow it to drop into his mind like a stone into a still lake. It will then work its effect on him. Some ancient but still well-used koans are:

What is the sound of one hand clapping?

Ummon said, 'Look! This world is vast and wide. Why do you put on your priest's robe at the sound of the bell?'

Master Gettan said to a monk, 'Keichu made a cart whose wheels had a hundred spokes. Take both front and rear wheels away and remove the axle: then what will it be?'

At regular intervals – once a week or once a month – the pupil goes for sanzen, an interview with the roshi (master), when he will be asked to demonstrate his understanding of the koan assigned to him. This must usually be done without explanation, although words can be employed, for direct pointing is what is requested. The roshi will reply in the same way, sometimes with a casual comment, sometimes with a whack from his stick, sometimes with a roar, sometimes with silence. Often the monk is in a state of tense expectation, and the roshi, an accurate judge of character, can give his pupil just the nudge he needs to break through his mental barriers.

Such a training is entirely at the discretion of individual roshis, and the rise and development of Zen is the record of these masters. One, Kuei-shan, said, 'One whose insight is the same as his teacher's lacks half of his teacher's power. Only one whose insight surpasses his teacher is worthy to be his heir.' This is an iron rule in Zen. According to Sokei-an, a modern master,

If a teacher hands the Dharma (the teaching) down to a pupil who is inferior to him, the Dharma will disappear in five hundred years. If the teacher picks a pupil whose view is just the same as his, Buddhism will go down while we watch. In the Zen school we must show some progress to our teacher. We must show him that we have something he doesn't and we must beat him down. Then the teacher gladly hands us the Dharma. It is never for so-called 'love' or 'because you have been so good to me. . . .' No! When a Zen teacher transmits his Dharma it is a championship fight – the disciple must knock him down, show him his attainment, knowledge and new information. Zen still exists because of this iron rule.

Before the female hawk will copulate with the male she flies for three days through the sky with the male pursuing her; only one who can overtake her can have her. The Zen master is like the female hawk, and the disciple is like the male. You must not forget this law.

Beginning in China and passing on to Korea, Vietnam and Japan, such was the way of transmission of 'enlightenment understanding' from master to pupil.

Little is known about the teaching of women in China, but in Japan women were trained at the Zen temple of Tokeiji, of which the first teacher was the nun, Shido, of the thirteenth century. Women were also accepted at Enkakuji Monastery, but only under stringent conditions, which included unmarried status and the passing of a test presented by the keeper of the gate. Zen nuns created and solved their own koans, and some of these are famous, such as the night interview of the nun Myotei who took off all her clothes before going to her teacher. The koan is: What is the real meaning of Myotei's coming naked for the night interview?

What follows is a description of the methods of six of the traditionally most important masters; on pp. 66–67 is a living master's dialogue on Zen with his pupil.

Hui Neng AD 637–714

'Depending upon nothing, you must find your own mind.' Hui Neng, an illiterate peasant boy, who was one day to become the great Sixth Patriarch of Zen, overheard these words being recited when he was gathering firewood. At once his mind became light and clear, illumined by the understanding that truth is not to be found in the shifting opinions of the world but in the only realizable thing there is: our own existence.

Hui Neng fully realized this in an instant (a different matter from reading about it) and later said he felt as though his hair stood on end. He questioned the man reciting, who told him that the line came from the Diamond Sutra of Buddhism, and that the full text said: 'All Bodhisattvas [Compassionate Ones], lesser or great, should develop a pure, lucid mind, not depending upon sound, flavour, touch, smell, or any quality. A Bodhisattva should develop a mind which clings to no thing whatsoever; and so he should establish it.'

'Go to the temple of the Fifth Zen Patriarch,' advised the man. 'That is where I got this sutra.' The Fifth Patriarch was a famous Zen master called Hung-jen, who always counselled both monks and laymen to observe the Diamond Sutra alone. So Hui

Neng set off, and after a journey of thirty days came to the temple on Yellow Plum Mountain where, with many others, he paid his respects to Master Hung-jen.

The Patriarch questioned him: 'Where have you come from and what do you want?'

Hui Neng replied, 'I am a commoner from near Canton in the south. I have come this long way to pay homage to the Master. I want only to become a Buddha; to realize the Buddha within myself.'

The Fifth Patriarch was struck by this and decided to give Hui Neng a test: 'You are from the south? That means you are a savage! How could you become a Buddha?'

Hui Neng answered, 'A human being can come from the north or the south, but there is neither north nor south about Buddhahood. The flesh of a savage is not the flesh of an abbot, but how can my Buddhahood be distinguished from yours?'

From that moment on, Hui Neng was accepted by Master Hung-jen as his disciple, but the master was in a strange dilemma. Zen at that time was still influenced by Indian Buddhism, with scholarly metaphysical debates obscuring the experience of direct awakening. Hung-jen knew that the well-read, polished, northern monks at his temple would make mincemeat of a little peasant boy from the south. So to save Hui Neng he sent him to the kitchens as a labourer, and for eight months Hui Neng contentedly split firewood and pounded rice.

One day the Fifth Patriarch summoned all the monks. He said, 'The question of birth and death is one of great importance to everyone in the world. You are seeking "merit" rather than enlightenment about birth and death. While your minds are deluded, "merit" is useless to save you. Go to your rooms and look into your own nature. With your original wisdom, each one of you make a short ode and come and read it to me. If you have found the great principle of Buddhism, I shall transmit the robe and the office to you and ordain you the Sixth Patriarch. This is urgent. Go at once. Do not delay. If you deliberate on wisdom, you cannot put it into use. A person who realizes his own nature, sees it the moment I mention it. If you are able to do this, you will realize it even under slashing swords of battle.'

Shen Hsiu, the head monk, was considered by everybody to be the most learned and thus most certain to win the honour. He himself was sure that he would have no competitors, but was less certain of his own understanding. So he composed an ode and in the middle of the night wrote it on the wall where the master must come across it. It read:

> *The body is the wisdom-tree,*
> *The mind is a bright mirror in a stand;*
> *Take care to wipe it all the time*
> *And allow no dust to cling.*

The master praised it courteously but in private told Shen Hsiu that it did not show spontaneity and that he had not yet found his own true nature and must try again. Hui Neng, in the meantime, had also composed an ode but had had to wait for somebody to write it down for him. It appeared the following morning, placed where Shen Hsiu's had been, and it read:

> *Fundamentally no wisdom-tree exists,*
> *Nor the stand of a mirror bright.*
> *Since all is Void from the beginning*
> *Where can the dust alight?*

Although it was generally admired, the master, fearing for Hui Neng, rubbed it out with his shoe, saying, 'This too is made by one who has not found his original nature.' But secretly he summoned Hui Neng to him in the middle of the night and gave him the insignia of his office, the Patriarch's robe and bowl, acknowledging him as his worthy successor. He said, 'If you are unaware of your real mind, learning Buddhism won't benefit you. If you are aware of your own mind, and see your original nature, you are one to be honoured with names of master, teacher, or Buddha. But you must hide the bright light of your understanding until the proper time arrives for you to speak.' Then, taking the oars of a small boat, he ferried Hui Neng across the river. Hui Neng set out southwards.

The master retired for five days, but then was forced to admit that Hui Neng had gone off with the robe and bowl. He hoped Hui Neng would have reached safety, but the jealous monks of his monastery, blindly believing that the transmission was material, determined to get the robe and bowl back. They pursued Hui Neng for two months, finally catching up with him on the top of a mountain. Their leader, Ming, was a learned student who had been practising meditation and reading the sutras for over twenty years and yet had understood nothing. To have the master's insignia taken off by a kitchen monk of only eight month's standing was too much. He went after Hui Neng, meaning to kill him. When Hui Neng saw him coming he flung the robe and bowl on to a great flat rock in front of him and said, 'This robe is the testimony of faith. No man can lift it by force.'

Ming came rushing up, thinking he would snatch the robe and bowl. But when he put his hands on the robe, said to have been worn by the Buddha himself, his conscience (for basically he was a good and honest man) awoke and suddenly brought him to a sense of the ignoble and wretched thing he was trying to do.

'It is the truth I want, and not the robe,' he admitted. 'Please, brother, help me to get rid of my ignorance.'

'If you want the truth,' said Hui Neng, 'cease running after things. Stop thinking about what is right and what is wrong but just see, at this moment, what your original face was like before your father and mother were born.'

Ming then saw the real truth of things, which previously he had beheld only in his imagination. He felt as though he had taken a deep drink of cold water and found his thirst quenched. Such an answer as Hui Neng's must be apprehended directly; it has no philosophical, intellectual or imaginative uses. Ming's mind, already opened by his conscience, was ready to drop away like a ripe plum from a tree, and his years of study were all repaid.

From then on, this statement of Hui Neng's was used as a question – a koan – to be given to beginners – 'What did your original face look like before your father and mother were born?' In Chinese law courts, koans were the 'orthodox writings which the sages and worthy men regarded as principles', and when the word koan is used for the teachings of the Buddha it means the same thing. As Miura and Sasaki have said,

The koans do not represent the private opinion of a single man but rather the highest principle, received alike by us and by the hundreds and thousands of Bodhisattvas of the three realms and the ten directions. This principle accords with the spiritual source, tallies with the mysterious meaning, destroys birth and death, and transcends the passions. It cannot be understood by logic; it cannot be transmitted in words; it cannot be explained in writing; it cannot be measured by reason. It is like the poisoned drum that kills all who hear it, or like the great fire that consumes all who come near it.

Hui Neng's koan is regarded as a basic pointer to one's own nature; it does away with all wonderings and speculations about the reality of existence. When a student is conditioned to forming conceptual answers to questions, it comes as a shock to find that there is no concept which can fit such a question. This very shock causes a doubt in his mind about his own assumptions, and that is the beginning of waking up.

Hui Neng's original face is empty of features; his ode is empty of mirrors. What is Hui Neng's emptiness? He said,

> When you hear me speak of emptiness, don't become attached to it, especially don't become attached to any idea of it. Merely "sitting" still with your mind vacant, you fall into notional emptiness.
>
> The boundless emptiness of the sky embraces the 'ten thousand things' of every shape and form – the sun, moon and stars; mountains and rivers; bushes and trees; bad people and good; good teachings and bad; heavens and hells. All these are included in emptiness.
>
> The emptiness of your original nature is just like this. It too embraces everything. To this aspect the word 'great' applies. All and everything is included in your own original nature.

Nothing has to be suppressed or annihilated: 'The infinite Ground is not for one second apart from the ordinary world of phenomena,' said Hui Neng. 'If you look for it as such, you will find yourself cut off from the ordinary relative world, which is as much your reality as everything else.'

After fifteen years of deliberate anonymity, Hui Neng judged the time ripe to reveal himself as the successor to the Fifth Patriarch. He became known as the greatest master of Zen, and, after his death, his works were put together and classified as a Buddhist sutra. He established the traditional practice of zazen, and defined it thus: 'In the midst of all good and evil, not a thought is aroused in the mind – this is called za. Seeing into one's Self-nature, not being moved at all – this is called zen.'

Such a way of meditation should be practised at all times and not just during formal sitting, he said. So much did he believe that it is the attitude of mind which is important, and not the physical posture, that he considered prolonged sitting as not much better than being dead, because of its implication that the truth can't be found when standing, walking or lying down. He said:

> *A living man who sits and does not lie down;*
> *A dead man who lies down and does not sit!*
> *After all these are just dirty skeletons.*

When he was seventy-six, he said to his monks: 'Gather round me. I have decided to leave this world.'

When the monks heard this they wept openly.

'For whom are you crying?' the master asked, 'Are you worrying about me because you think I don't know where I'm going? If I didn't know, I wouldn't be able to leave you this way. What you're really crying about is that *you* don't know where I'm going. If you actually knew, you couldn't possibly cry because you would be aware that the True-Nature is without birth or death, without going or coming.'

Lin-chi (Japanese
name Rinzai)
d. AD 866

Lin-chi is considered one of the most powerful masters in the entire history of Zen; and the school which he founded became the most influential of all the sects which arose after Hui Neng. He died in the ninth century; but up to the middle of the twelfth century, generation after generation of his followers were leading Zen masters. In the twelfth century his teaching was taken to Japan where it became the Rinzai School, one of the two major schools of Zen which still flourish there today.

During Lin-chi's lifetime China was constantly at war with fierce and savage invaders, Tartars and Turks from the west. The national spirit was strong and warrior-like, and Zen itself was characterized in those times by bluntness and forcefulness. Lin-chi's own methods of teaching were straightforward and dynamic. He had no compunction about using a blow if he thought his pupil needed jerking out of a wordy thought-rut, and he became notorious for his rough treatment. In ordinary circumstances such behaviour would be merely insulting; but in Zen teaching it became a way of opening up the mind beyond all intellection.

When Lin-chi was asked a philosophical or metaphysical question, his reply was a blow. What could be the answer to this? The pupil could not respond in terms of logic, nor could he turn to any traditional teaching for help; he had nothing to lean on in any direction. He was suddenly adrift in a world without reason, adrift from the usual sequence of thoughts to which he had believed himself bound. But if he were sincere in his question, his entire being intent on knowing the answer, there would be an abandonment of all his former thinking, and his mind would open up to the direct experience of his own nature.

Lin-chi was a great smasher of religious conventions. He detested the roundabout way in which clear truth was treated by philosophers and learned scholars. His own methods emphasized spontaneity and absolute freedom. He said:

Many students come to see me from all over the place. Many of them are not free from their entanglement with objective things. I treat them right on the spot. If their trouble is due to grasping hands, I strike there. If their trouble is a loose mouth, I strike them there. If their trouble is hidden behind their eyes, it is there I strike. So far I have not found anyone who can set himself free. This is because they have all been caught up in the useless ways of the old masters. As for me, I do not have one only method which I give to everyone, but I relieve whatever the trouble is and set men free.

Friends, I tell you this: there is no Buddha, no spiritual path to follow, no training and no realization. What are you so feverishly running after? Putting a head on top of your own head, you blind idiots? Your head is right where it should be. The trouble lies in your not believing in yourselves enough. Because you don't believe in yourselves you are knocked here and there by all the conditions in which you find yourselves. Being enslaved and turned around by objective situations, you have no freedom whatever, you are not masters of yourselves. Stop turning to the outside and don't be attached to my words either. Just cease clinging to the past and hankering after the future. This will be better than ten years' pilgrimage.

Lin-chi's name first became known when he was a young monk studying under Master Huang Po. In Huang Po's temple of some five hundred monks, Lin-chi went quite unnoticed for his first three years. In the morning he worked in the fields with the others, in the afternoon he meditated, and in the evenings he helped in the kitchens or prepared baths for the older monks. In all those three years he was obscure and unknown, like a young undergraduate in a big university.

But the head monk, Mu Chou, had observed him and had noticed his particularly pure and single-minded way of doing things, so that when he was eating he ate and when he was meditating he meditated. His whole self was in accord with whatever action he was engaged in, with no thought of self-interest or possessiveness or pride, so that his actions were like gold and not alloy. But because he was so honest and straightforward he never had anything to ask the master, and would not push himself forward for no reason.

One day, Mu Chou, who wanted the master to notice Lin-chi, told him to ask the master a question. Since, however, he had none of his own to ask, Mu Chou advised him to ask what the fundamental principle of Buddhism was. When Lin-chi stood before Huang Po and asked him this, Huang Po hit him with his six-foot pole. Again Lin-chi asked the question and again he was hit. And a third time too.

He decided there must be some barrier in his mind which prevented him from seeing the truth, and he determined to leave the monastery and become a beggar in order that he might learn from ordinary life that which was not clear to him in a monastic setting. He told Mu Chou of his plans, and Mu Chou told Huang Po, adding, 'Be kind to this young man. A huge tree might be carved from him which would some day shelter many people.'

When Lin-chi went to take his leave of the master, Huang Po said, 'There is no need to travel far. Just go to Master Ta Yu. He will teach you what is meant.'

So Lin-chi went to Ta Yu's monastery and with great hope told him all that had happened. Ta Yu said, 'Why, Huang Po was as kind to you as your own grandmother. Why have you come here, asking me about your faults?'

At these words, enlightenment burst upon Lin-chi and suddenly he felt as though his eyes were fully open. Up till then he had always thought of Buddhism as a powerful teaching separate from himself. Now he saw that it was only an idea in his mind. He at once became a man. Until then he had been like an animal, having eyes and ears but not using them as his own. He had been wholly identified with the outer world, the world of people and objects and events, and his eyes and ears had belonged there too. Now, in a flash, he let go of the world and in that moment he knew existence as it is in itself, and the unreality of all words about it. Huang Po's stick had pointed to the truth of his own being, whereas his own question about Buddhism had sprung from illusion.

He burst out: 'Ah, I see what I did not see before.' Then he added, 'From the first there never was anything in Huang Po's Buddhism.'

Such a thing to admit after three years of humble work in Huang Po's monastery! But now he realized the true and liberating kindness of Huang Po.

Ta Yu guessed what had happened and decided to test Lin-chi. He grabbed him and said: 'You bed-wetting urchin! Only a moment ago you were asking me whether you were wrong or not and now you say there is nothing in Huang Po's Buddhism. What have you seen? Say now! Spit it out!'

At once Lin-chi poked Ta Yu sharply in the ribs three times. Pushing him off, Ta Yu said, 'Go back to Huang Po. He is your teacher. All this is his business and does not concern me.'

At the sight of Lin-chi returning to the monastery, Huang Po said, 'This fellow's coming and going will never end.' To Lin-chi he said, 'What are you doing back here, you oaf? You'll never find the truth travelling about like this.'

Lin-chi said, 'You're so kind, just like my old grandmother. That's why I've come back', and he stood beside Huang Po in the attitude of a monk who intends to stay with a master, hands on his chest.

'Where have you been?' asked Huang Po. In those days some monks might have answered that question poetically – 'I have come riding on the wind' – but Lin-chi was unconcerned with such effects and told him exactly what had happened in a straightforward way.

'Just wait till Ta Yu comes here,' said Huang Po, who was really delighted. 'I'll give that blabbermouth a real beating.'

'Why wait?' said Lin-chi, 'You have it [Reality] all now,' and he hit Huang Po.

Huang Po was secretly very amused, but he preserved his master's attitude and shouted, 'A madman! He's come back to pull the tiger's whiskers.'

Lin-chi thundered a great shout of 'HO!'

Huang Po called an attendant and said, 'Drag this lunatic away from here and drive him into the meditation hall.' He did not say out of the temple but into the hall, so he had decided to keep the madman.

Lin-chi's 'Ho' became famous and is still used by Rinzai masters. In Japanese it has become 'Kwatz', and, although it has no exact meaning, it conveys a great deal. It is used to sweep clear the student's mind and to free him from dualistic, ego-centred thoughts. Lin-chi distinguished four kinds of Ho: 'Sometimes it is like the jewel sword of the Vajra [Thunderbolt] king; sometimes it is like the golden-haired lion crouching on the ground; sometimes it is like a grass-tipped decoy pole; and sometimes it is no Ho at all.'

After ten years of further practice, Lin-chi took up residence in a temple to the north, and many disciples came to him. His teaching was earthy and matter-of-fact, inspiring courage in his students to have faith that their natural, spontaneous functioning was the true Buddha-mind. To be in this pure state of being was to stop obstructing or blocking anything. In this way, to be free from attachment did not mean having no feelings, or having no sensations of hunger, pain, etc. It meant entering into everything with the whole self, nothing held back, free to be entirely at one with any circumstance. This, for Lin-chi, was the sublime way to live ordinary life; and he was frequently exasperated that his students looked for anything else. They had come from everywhere to search for deliverance from the world, he told them; but if delivered from the world, where could they go? His advice was to live as any man lives, but to do it without blind, enslaving desire.

'When it's time to get dressed, put on your clothes. When you must walk, then walk. When you must sit, then sit. Just be your ordinary self in ordinary life, unconcerned in seeking for Buddhahood. When you're tired, lie down. The fool will laugh at you but the wise man will understand.'

Zen is not concerned with the idea of Buddha or God but with the Reality of the human being. The true human being does not strive for what he can get out of life but for what life is in itself, and he lives according to this knowledge. Then he is free from wrong ideas about things and can act in harmony with the universe at all times.

Lin-chi said: 'The Self far transcends all things. Even if heaven and earth tumbled down, I would have no misgivings. Even though all the Buddhas in ten directions appeared before me, I would not rejoice. Even though the three hells appeared before me, I would have no fear. Why is it like this? Because there is nothing I dislike.'

Dogen 1200–53   Rinzai (Lin-chi) Zen became popular in Japan in the twelfth century, but it did not satisfy everyone. Dogen, the founder of the large Soto sect still flourishing in Japan, was of a different, less radical temperament. He came of a noble family, but his childhood was far from happy, for his father died when he was three and his mother when he was seven. Dogen's mind was deeply affected by their deaths, which he saw, even when very young, as a revelation of the transient nature of life. At the age of thirteen his greatest wish was granted, and he was allowed to become a Buddhist monk. By the time he was fourteen, however, he had become troubled by a deep doubt concerning the Buddhist teaching. If, as the scriptures maintained, all human beings are born with Buddha-nature, why is it that it is so hard to realize it?

Dogen had not then seen the truth of Zen, which is that the hardness lies not so much in acquiring training as in dropping preconceptions; that only the practice of a particular awareness will bring you to the Reality of yourself, an awareness which takes you out of the realm of definition to a place where you can no longer point to yourself as 'I'. As long as you can still see yourself as an object, it is not your true self you are observing. The reality of life goes beyond all its definitions. The word 'fire' can never convey the actual touch of a flame, and in the same way no classification of oneself can ever reach the living Reality. Buddhists believe that this underlying, subjective Reality is the essential nature of everything, and so it can never be lost, only lost sight of. It goes by many names – the Self, Buddha-nature, Suchness, Nirvana – and in Christianity it is sometimes called the Ground of God or the Immanence of God.

The young Dogen had not realized that the 'I', composed of all its conditions, such as race, class or sex – this 'I' which is related horizontally to the world and which has only a social appearance and only a worldly evaluation – is not the whole Self. It was to take him years to discover that few people live from the real life of the Self, and that most need training and practice to find their own Reality because the horizontal 'I' is entangled in so many needs and desires.

After much enquiry Dogen eventually discovered a Rinzai master, Eisai, who illumined his mind about his great doubt. Only the deluded think in such dualistic terms as Buddha-nature and human nature, he told Dogen. When enlightenment comes, there is no consciousness of the split between oneself and Buddha-nature. Dogen's deep acceptance of this answer gave him satori, and for the remaining few months of Eisai's life he stayed with him as his disciple. After his death he remained with Eisai's successor, Myozen, for eight years.

But still, in spite of having received his inka (the seal of a master) during this time, Dogen felt that some great understanding was lacking. When he was twenty-four he went off with Myozen to China to study Zen further, away from the Japanese Rinzai school. Under Master Ju-ching he practised zazen constantly. But he fell into the error of sitting in a quietist way – leading to the 'vacant' or 'notional' emptiness which Hui Neng had condemned – until one day he heard the master, making his early round of inspection, scold another monk because he was dozing. The master said, 'The practice of zazen is the dropping away of body and mind. What do you think dozing is going to accomplish?'

When he overheard these words Dogen suddenly saw the truth: Zazen was not a mere sitting still, it was the dynamic opening up of the Self to its own Reality directly, by letting go of all ideas about life. When life is experienced without the ego intervening, the experience is that of its true and numinous nature. After this insight, he said:

Mind and body dropped off; dropped off mind and body! This state should be experienced by everyone; it is like piling fruit into a basket without a bottom, like pouring water into a bowl with a pierced hole; however much you may pile or pour you cannot fill it up. When this is realized the pail bottom is broken through.

But while there is still a trace of conceptualism which makes you say 'I have this understanding' or 'I have that realization', you are still playing with unrealities.

Later he went to the master's room and lit a stick of incense before prostrating himself. The master asked, 'Why have you lit a stick of incense?' He did not really need to ask, because Dogen's appearance revealed his satori; but by putting such a simple question he could judge the level of Dogen's understanding.

'I have experienced the dropping away of body and mind,' answered Dogen.

Ju-ching saw that Dogen's enlightenment was real.

'You have indeed dropped body and mind,' he said.

Used to fierce challenge, Dogen was astonished at the master's quick acknowledgment of his state. 'Don't sanction me so easily,' he protested.

'I am not sanctioning you easily.'

Still puzzled, Dogen persisted, 'What makes you say that you haven't sanctioned me easily?'

'Body and mind dropped away,' replied Ju-ching.

At once reassured, Dogen prostrated himself before his master as a deep gesture of respect and gratitude.

'That's dropping dropped!' added Ju-ching.

On his return to Japan after four years in China, Dogen was asked what kind of realization he had obtained abroad. He replied, 'I have come back empty-handed. I have realized only that the eyes are horizontal and the nose is vertical.' He came back with nothing to show, no scriptures or holy learning, not even 'a hair of Buddhism'. From this dropped-away, empty-handed clarity came the great Soto sect of Japan.

Dogen set up his own meditation hall in Kyoto. To the many monks who came to him he taught a way of sitting, shikan-taza, which has remained the basis of all Soto Zen up to the present. It is a unique coalescence of means and end in which the pupil sits in the firm conviction that his sitting is the actualization of his timeless Buddha-nature, or Being, and at the same time he sits in complete faith that the moment of realization will come when he will unmistakably know this pure Being. So there is no need for him to strive self-consciously for satori; it is bound to come as a result of this practice. On the other hand he must not lapse into mere sitting but must maintain for as long as he can the particular taut awareness of shikan-taza, shikan meaning 'nothing but' while ta means 'to hit' and za 'to sit'.

Dogen gave detailed instructions for right bodily posture and correct temper of mind during meditation:

> In doing zazen it is desirable to have a quiet room. You should be temperate in eating and drinking, forsaking all delusive relationships. Setting everything aside, think of neither good nor evil, right nor wrong. Thus, having stopped the various functions of your mind, give up even the idea of becoming a Buddha. This holds true not only for zazen but for all your daily actions.
>
> Usually a thick square mat is put on the floor where you sit and a round cushion on top of that. You may sit in either the full or half lotus position. In the former, first put your right foot on your left thigh and then your left foot on your right thigh. In the latter, only put your left foot on your right thigh. Your clothing should be worn loosely but neatly. Next, put your right hand on your left foot and your left palm on the right palm, the tips of the thumbs lightly touching. Sit upright, leaning to neither left nor right, front nor back. Your ears should be on the same

plane as your shoulders and your nose in line with your navel. Your tongue should be placed against the roof of your mouth and your lips and teeth closed firmly. With your eyes kept continuously open, breathe quietly through your nostrils. Finally, having regulated your body and mind in this way, take a deep breath, sway your body to left and right, then sit firmly as a rock. Think of non-thinking. How is this done? By thinking beyond non-thinking and thinking. This is the very basis of zazen.

Zazen is not a 'step-by-step' meditation. Rather it is simply the easy and pleasant practice of a Buddha, the realization of the Buddha's wisdom. The truth appears, there being no delusion. If you understand this you are completely free, like a dragon that has found water or a tiger reclining on a mountain. The supreme law will then appear of itself, and you will be free of weariness and confusion.

At the completion of zazen move your body slowly and stand up calmly. Do not move violently.

The purpose of such a precise posture as Dogen describes is twofold. First, the full lotus gives a wide, solid, physical base, and when both knees touch the mat there is absolute body stability. Second, the immobile and rock-like posture of the body slows down the chatter of the mind and brings stillness and tranquillity.

In Soto Zen today the student is usually given a breathing practice to concentrate his mind. For beginners, the easiest way is to count incoming and outgoing breaths up to ten and then return to one and start again. The value of this practice is that the discriminating mind has nothing to feed on, nor is there anything for reasoning to get hold of. Nevertheless, fleeting thoughts will come and go as they naturally do, and Dogen's advice was to take each as it comes and place it in the palm of the hand.

When the student is ready for the more advanced shikan-taza, or practice-enlightenment zazen, the mind-support of breathing practice is left behind. The mind must now become as firmly seated as the body, peacefully unhurried and yet wholly resolute and without a trace of quietism; alert and stretched like a bow-string in an effortless concentrated awareness. Dogen likened this easy and yet intensely watchful awareness to the vigilance of a swordsman in a duel. Such an attitude of mind is unmoved by the world about it: it is itself the unmoving centre of all movement. 'Abandoning thinking and doing,' said Dogen, 'is nothing other than every form of doing and acting.'

Dogen was perhaps the first Zen master to comprehend, or at any rate the first to teach, that life is one, all of a piece; that when we split it up into bits, some of which are fascinating, others boring, yet others important or not important to us personally, etc., we are in fact losing the flow of life altogether. By attempting to dominate events we strand ourselves on false islands of permanence, seeing ourselves as stationary while 'life' rushes past. Dogen taught that every moment and every action, however insignificant, should be seen as the actual realization of Buddhahood. There are no means to an end, because the end is now.

To realize this moment now became the great aim of the Soto school. Sitting in zazen was not a way of aiming at satori or anything else; it was entering the flow of each moment by unblocking the mind from the concepts of past, present and future. In his great work, the Shobogenzo, Dogen made it clear that to fix all one's hopes on a goal is pointless. He said:

When a fish swims, it swims on and on, and there is no end to the water. When a bird flies, it flies on and on, and there is no end to the sky. There was never a fish that swam out of the water or a bird that flew out of the sky. When they need just a little water or sky, they use just a little; when they need a lot, they use a lot. Thus, they use all of it in every moment, and in every place they have perfect freedom.

Yet if there were a bird that first wanted to examine the size of the sky, or a fish that first wanted to examine the extent of the water, and then tried to fly or swim, it would never find its way. When we find where we are at this moment, then practice follows, and this is the realization of the truth. For the place, the way, is neither large nor small, neither self nor other. It has never existed before, and it is not coming into existence now. It simply is as it is.

Hakuin
AD 1686–1769

In the same way as Hui Neng gave to Zen its Chinese flavour, Hakuin created a Japanese Rinzai Zen. His tremendous vigour and the versatility of his teaching gave Zen a new structure. Yet in spite of all the energy he poured into life – he was not only a formidable Zen master but also a renowned painter, poet and sculptor – in spite of all his great works he remains one of the most vulnerable, likeable and human of the masters. As an old man, he would sit in the fields with the peasants, perched on the furrows while they planted the seed, and talk to them of Zen.

He was brought up in a deeply religious family in a village at the foot of Mount Fuji. His father was a samurai and his mother was a devotee of the ecstatic Nichiren sect of Buddhism. Hakuin, who was a sensitive boy and gifted with such a remarkable memory that at the age of four he could recite three hundred of the local songs, longed to become a monk, and at fifteen was allowed to enter a small Zen temple in his native village. Shortly afterwards he was invited to continue his training at a larger monastery nearby, and he was there until he was nineteen. It was then that a great doubt entered his mind. It concerned the death of a Chinese Zen master called Ganto. This master stood up to a gang of robbers, and when all the other monks fled from the temple, he remained. One of the brigands ran a spear through him and although his facial expression did not change, he gave a great cry as he died, which was heard for miles around.

Hakuin was deeply depressed at this account of human frailty. If even such a spiritual man as Ganto could be overcome by fear and pain, what hope was there for an ordinary seeker like himself? He considered giving up Zen altogether and becoming a poet. Then one day he saw the books of a temple library being brought out into the sun for the customary annual airing, and, closing his eyes, he picked up one book. He found it was a study of Zen and it fell open at a chapter relating how one Abbot Jimyo, meditating while others slept, himself kept falling asleep. To keep awake, he pierced his thigh with a gimlet. From this story Hakuin found new courage to continue his meditation. After four years of intense and devoted sitting, meditating on the koan of whether a dog has Buddha nature, he passed into a state which he compared to

freezing in an ice-field extending thousands of miles, and within myself there was a sense of utmost transparency. There was no going forward, no slipping backward; I was like an idiot, like an imbecile, and there was nothing but the koan. Though I attended the lectures given by the master, they sounded like a discussion going on somewhere in a distant hall, many yards away. Sometimes my sensation was that of one flying in the air. Several days passed in this state, when one evening a temple-bell struck which upset the whole thing. It was like smashing an ice-basin, or pulling down a house made of jade. When I suddenly awoke again, I found that I myself was Ganto, the old master, and that all through the shifting changes of time not a bit of my personality was lost. Whatever doubts and indecisions I had before were completely dissolved like a piece of thawing ice. I called out loudly, 'How wonderful! How wonderful! There is no birth and death from which one has to escape, nor is there any supreme knowledge after which one has to strive.'

Hakuin saw that his old ideas of Ganto's cry were not based on a living person but only on concepts of how Zen masters should behave. His elation at this discovery and at his whole satori-like experience led him to believe that he was now enlightened – in fact he was sure that nobody had had such a deep satori for hundreds of years. But the master of his monastery remained lukewarm about it. Disappointed, Hakuin visited a number of other masters, hoping to get their recognition, but no one was willing to give it; undoubtedly he was making far too much of it and therefore it had not gone deep enough. Finally, with his pride distinctly humbled, he was advised to practise under a stern master, Shoju.

When he arrived with his story of enlightenment, Shoju asked him, 'Tell me, what has your koan accomplished?' Hakuin rapturously replied, 'The universe dropped off! Dropped off! Not a spot whatsoever to take hold of!' As soon as he had given that reply, Shoju grasped Hakuin's nose and gave it a tweak. 'How is it that I have a bit of the universe here?' he asked, laughing. Then he let Hakuin go and abused him, 'You dead monk in a cave! What self-satisfaction!'

Absolute confidence must be placed in a master if his instruction is to succeed, and Hakuin was depressed by this reception. But he remained doggedly convinced that he had had a great satori. One evening he presented his latest understanding in his earnest way to old Shoju, who was cooling himself on the verandah. 'Stuff and nonsense,' said the master. Hakuin, cut to the quick, sarcastically mimicked the master, 'Stuff and nonsense', whereupon Shoju seized him and pushed him off the verandah. It was the rainy season, and poor Hakuin rolled in mud and water. But he got up, pulled himself together and made a reverent bow to the master, who peered at him, remarking, 'O you denizen of a dark cave!'

Hakuin was now desperate and on the point of leaving Shoju. Then one day his real illumination came. He was visiting the village on the daily food-begging round and came to a house where an old woman refused to give him any rice. He was concentrating so intensely on his situation that he barely noticed her refusal and went on standing in front of the house as though nothing had been said to him. This infuriated the old woman, who thought he was ignoring her words, and she struck him with the heavy broom she was using. The blow crashed through his monk's hat and knocked him to the ground. When he came to his senses again, his obsession was gone and everything was lucidly clear to him. Feeling boundless joy he returned to the monastery, where the master immediately recognized his state and said, 'Tell me quickly how it is with you.' Hakuin described everything and Shoju tenderly stroked his back, saying, 'Now you have it, now you have it.'

Shoju's treatment of Hakuin is well known. His harshness was a necessary measure to correct Hakuin's insistence on his own understanding. By dwelling on his thoughts, Hakuin had fallen into a deep rut. On such occasions no intellectual arguments can pull a man out. The only thing that can rescue him is a strong internal movement which can sweep aside all that is dwelling cosily in his mind. When Hakuin was roughly knocked down by the old woman's broom, he had arrived at such an intense pitch of mental concentration that the blow woke him up from the depths of his obsession and gave him an understanding beyond logical comprehension.

Later, Hakuin taught that a koan can lead to enlightenment but only when such tremendous power of effort is used that the Great Doubt, as he called it, is aroused:

> If you take up one koan and investigate it without ceasing, your thoughts will die and your ego-demands will be destroyed. It is as though a vast abyss opened up in front of you, with no place to put your hands and feet. You face death, and your heart feels as though it were fire. Then suddenly you are one with the koan, and body and mind are let go. . . . This is known as seeing into one's own nature. You must push forward relentlessly, and with the help of this great concentration you will penetrate without fail to the infinite source of your own nature.

Now that he had won his harsh master's recognition, Hakuin decided to go back to Shoin-ji, the little temple in the village of his birth. But because of the great strains he had been through, he found himself undergoing a severe nervous breakdown. 'My courage failed and I was in an attitude of constant fear. I felt spiritually exhausted, night and day seeing dreams, my armpits always wet with sweat and my eyes full of tears. I cast about in every direction consulting famous teachers and doctors, but all their devices availed not at all.'

He was advised to seek out an old recluse, Master Hakuyu, who lived high up on a mountainside. After a long and arduous climb, Hakuin found the master meditating in a cave filled with soft grass and screened by a reed curtain. The master recognized his condition at once, calling it the Zen illness, as it came about by overconcentration on truth and consequent loss of the vital rhythms of proper spiritual advance. He advised Hakuin to let go all his doubts and to meditate instead on the channels of the body and in particular on the tanden, the centre of feeling which is said to be situated just below the navel. He was also to visualize an exquisite lotion filtering down from the crown of his head to his feet and then filling up the lower half of his body with great warmth. These psycho-physical practices, which Hakuin tackled with his usual immense vigour, succeeded in ridding his mind of its stress, and he recovered completely.

From then on, Hakuin never looked back. His experiences of satori deepened, and he began to teach many disciples in his old temple of Shoin-ji, which he rebuilt with his own hands. He taught his pupils to deepen their understanding by means of a graded system of koans, and he created many koans of his own, the most famous being 'What is the sound of one hand clapping?'

When they had attained illumination, his pupils were to consider this a new beginning, and were to go on with the quest for the Reality of life through deeper and deeper penetration into meditation. Hakuin said:

> Now, if asked what is this spirit of meditation, I reply that it is to have a sincerely benevolent and sympathetic heart at all times, whether one is talking or wagging one's elbow when writing, whether one is moving or resting, whether one's luck is good or bad, whether one is in honour or shame, or in gain or loss, in right or wrong – bundling all these things up into one verse heading and concentrating your energy with the force of an iron rock under the navel and lower part of the abdomen – this is the spirit of meditation.
>
> If you have this spirit then, by that very fact, your two-edged sword will be your

meditation table, placed always before you. The saddle you ride on will be the cushion on which you sit in meditation. The hills, the streams, the plains will be the floor of your meditation hall. The four corners of the earth and its ten directions, the height and depth of the universe will be to you the great 'cave' in which you are performing your meditation – they will be, in very truth, the substance of your real self.

Hakuin was the first master to systematize Zen training. His advice to his students on attitudes of mind was so pithy and direct that it was said to be like a mother talking to her children:

> For the study of Zen there are three essential requirements. The first is a great root of faith; the second is a great ball of doubt; the third is great tenacity of purpose. A man who lacks any one of these is like a three-legged kettle with one broken leg.
>
> What is a root of faith? It is nothing less than the belief that every man possesses his own intrinsic nature into which he can attain insight, and that there is a Fundamental Principle which can be completely penetrated. Just this. But even though he has sincere faith, if a man does not bring concentrated doubt to bear upon the koans that are difficult to pass through, he cannot get to the bottom of them and penetrate them all completely. And even though this ball of doubt be firmly solidified, if it is not succeeded by great tenacity of purpose, it will not finally be shattered.
>
> The study of Zen is like drilling wood to get fire. The wisest course is to forge straight ahead without stopping. If you pause at the first sign of heat, and then again as soon as the first wisp of smoke arises, even though you go on drilling for years you will never see a spark of fire. My native place is close to the seashore, barely a hundred paces from the beach. Suppose a man of my village is concerned because he does not know the flavour of sea water, and wants to go and taste it for himself. If he turns back after having taken only a few steps, or even if he retreats after having taken a hundred steps, in either case when will he ever know the ocean's bitter, salty taste? But, though a man comes from as far as the mountains of Koshu, if he goes straight ahead without stopping, within a few days he will reach the shore, and the moment he dips the tip of one finger into the sea and licks it, he will instantly know the taste of the waters of the distant oceans and the nearby seas, of the southern beaches and the northern shores, in fact of all the sea water in the world.

Shunryu Suzuki 1905–71

Shunryu Suzuki was a member of the Soto Zen sect founded by Dogen. Little is known of his life before he arrived in America in 1958, although his chief disciple and teaching heir, Richard Baker, relates that Suzuki was the son of a Zen master – Soto priests frequently marry – and while still a boy began his Zen training under Gyokujun, a famous Soto master of the time and a disciple of Suzuki's own father. When he was about thirty – an early age in Zen terms – Suzuki himself was given the seal of the teaching and acknowledged a master. He was put in charge of a number of Zen temples and a monastery. The nature of Soto Zen is non-violent, and during the Second World War Suzuki became the leader of a pacifist movement in Japan, which cannot have been easy.

In 1958 he was invited to San Francisco to take charge of the Japanese Soto sect there. Although he intended to stay only a year or two, eventually he decided to remain, having found there a true source of discipleship. He called the American mind 'beginner's mind', because of the openness to Zen that he found – an openness which goes with lack of preconceptions – and because of the trust which Americans put in him that Zen could profoundly enhance their lives. Soon after his arrival a group of Americans gathered about him, and Zen Center in San Francisco was established, where sixty students could live and many more attend daily. Then Zen Mountain Center was built at Tassajara Springs and became the first Zen monastery outside Asia.

Zen Mind, Beginner's Mind, on which this chapter is based, is a published collection of Suzuki's informal talks, and is especially helpful to those encountering Zen for the first time. He divides his talks into three groups: right practice, right attitude and right understanding. In Rinzai Zen that particular order would perhaps be reversed, but the difference is only one of emphasis.

What is real beginner's mind? There are many people who at some time have received in a flash an unforgettable experience of wonder and delight when the ego is forgotten and the world seems clear and numinous. The cause may be as trivial as the touch of a hand, or as majestic as the sun setting over the ocean, but whatever its nature, surrender to its enchantment never fails to bring a glimpse of what Suzuki calls 'original mind', when the mind knows totality and is not divided. 'Beginner's mind' is close to the transcendent boundlessness of original mind, because it is not full of pre-formed judgments but is open and alert and marvellously empty to receive all possibilities. Thomas Traherne, an English mystic, once described the sheer joy of beginner's mind when he said:

> You never enjoy the world aright till the sea itself flows in your veins, till you are clothed with the heavens and crowned with the stars and perceive yourself to be the sole heir of the whole world, and more than so, because men are in it who are every one sole heirs as well as you. Till you can sing and rejoice and delight in God, as misers do in gold, and kings in sceptres, you never enjoy the world.

So speaks the Self-sufficient, or God-sufficient 'beginner' who owns nothing in the way of mental baggage and who is true to himself and at one with all life. Suzuki points out that to be a beginner is the real secret of living: however much we may know and understand and achieve, it is essential to resume, ever again, the shining unknowing of the beginner. It is the secret of 'right practice', he says: the first part of Zen. And how does one practise Zen?

> Now I would like to talk about our zazen posture. When you sit in the full lotus position, your left foot is on your right thigh and your right foot is on your left thigh. When we cross our legs like this, even though we have a right leg and a left leg, they have become one. The position expresses the oneness of duality: not two and not one. This is the most important teaching: not two, and not one. Our body and mind are not two and not one. If you think your body and mind are two, that is wrong; if you think that they are one, that is also wrong. Our body and mind are both two *and* one. We usually think that if something is not one, it is more than one; if it is not singular, it is plural. But in actual experience, our life is not only plural, but also singular. Each one of us is both dependent and independent.
>
> After some years we will die. If we just think that it is the end of our life, this will

be the wrong understanding. But, on the other hand, if we think that we do not die, this is also wrong. We die, and we do not die. This is the right understanding. Some people may say that our mind or soul exists forever, and it is only our physical body which dies. But this is not exactly right, because both mind and body have their end. But at the same time it is also true that they exist eternally. And even though we say mind and body, they are actually two sides of one coin. This is the right understanding. So when we take this posture it symbolizes this truth. When I have the left foot on the right side of my body, and the right foot on the left side of my body, I do not know which is which. So either may be the left or the right side.

Suzuki goes on to explain that sitting with the spine straight, ears and shoulders in one line, and chin tucked in as though 'supporting the sky with your head', is to enter the proper Buddhist state of being – the body and mind right here: nothing to seek, nothing to attain, simply being where you are, in the moment:

These forms are not the means of obtaining the right state of mind. To take this posture is itself to have the right state of mind. There is no need to obtain some special state of mind.

The most important thing is to own your own physical body. If you slump, you will lose yourself. Your mind will be wandering about somewhere else; you will not be in your body. This is not the way. We must exist right here, right now! This is the key point. You must have your own body and mind. Everything should exist in the right place, in the right way. Then there is no problem. If the microphone I use when I speak exists somewhere else, it will not serve its purpose. When we have our body and mind in order, everything else will exist in the right place, in the right way.

An important key to mind-presence is good breathing:

When we practise zazen our mind always follows our breathing. When we inhale, the air comes into the inner world. When we exhale, the air goes to the outer world. The inner world is limitless, and the outer world is also limitless. We say 'inner world' or 'outer world', but actually there is just one whole world. In this limitless world, our throat is like a swinging door. If you think, 'I breathe', the 'I' is extra. There is no you to say 'I'. What we call 'I' is just a swinging door which moves when we inhale and when we exhale. It just moves; that is all. When your mind is pure and calm enough to follow this movement, there is nothing: no 'I', no world, no mind or body; just a swinging door.

Suzuki explains that the swinging-door movement brings awareness not of the little ego but of universal or Buddha nature. In this awareness the usual dualistic way in which we regard life – good times and bad times, this and that, I and you – are seen as they really are; expressions of one indivisible existence. '"You" means to be aware of the universe in the form of you, and "I" means to be aware of it in the form of I. You and I are just swinging doors. This kind of understanding is necessary. This should not even be called understanding; it is actually the true experience of life through Zen practice.'

Because we live superficially and do not penetrate deeply enough in our understanding, we become trapped by the power of names. We believe that the label is the thing itself, although it is only man-devised and has no lasting substance. A label divides and isolates, whereas the swinging-door awareness, of the one existence behind the many names, unites and integrates: 'Night-time and daytime are not different. The same thing is sometimes called night-time, sometimes called daytime. They are one thing.'

Yet we must not cling to oneness as though it too were a thing. The one meaning is expressed in every variation – every blade of grass and grain of sand – and when, in zazen, we settle down into ourselves, the amazing and intricate scenery of our own life can be known afresh and with deeper understanding of its variations. The practice of looking in this way is the 'right attitude' which is the theme of the second part of Suzuki's book.

> Of course, whatever we do is the expression of our true nature, but without this practice it is difficult to realize. It is our human nature to be active and the nature of every existence. As long as we are alive, we are always doing something. But as long as you think, 'I am doing this', or 'I have to do this', or 'I must attain something special', you are actually not doing anything. When you give up, when you no longer want something, or when you do not try to do anything special, then you do something. When there is no gaining idea in what you do, then you do something.

But how can we practise such an attitude at all times, even when cooking a meal or catching a bus? Whether we catch the bus or see it go off without us, the *inner* feeling will be the same if we are prepared to accept that the moments of waiting for the next bus have their own particular reality and are not just the object for our impatience.

This does not mean that we must try to avoid emotions such as repugnance or dislike. 'Although everything has Buddha-nature,' says Dogen, 'we love flowers and we do not care for weeds'. In his third section on 'right understanding', Suzuki says that both love of beauty and dislike of ugliness are natural to human beings and are what he calls 'Buddha's activity'. We should realize this, so that when we feel love we can know it as a less obsessively personal emotion: 'We should not attach to love alone. We should accept hate. We should accept weeds, despite how we feel about them. If you do not care for them, do not love them; if you love them, then love them.'

By this activity of accepting things in their own existence and their own unique being, the problems of life begin to press in upon us less. It is because we usually insist upon emphasizing one particular aspect that we run into trouble, but when each moment is itself totally real and balanced there is a feeling of being at one with all things and every situation:

> This kind of experience is something beyond our thinking. In the thinking realm there is a difference between oneness and variety; but in actual experience, variety and unity are the same. Because you create some idea of unity or variety, you are caught by the idea. And you have to continue the endless thinking, although actually there is no need to think.

Seung Sahn
Soen-sa b. 1927

Seung Sahn, known by his pupils as Soen-sa, was born at Seun Choen, in what is now North Korea. His parents were Protestant Christians. In *Dropping Ashes on the*

Buddha, a published collection of Soen-sa's talks, letters and dialogues, Stephen Mitchell, his disciple and editor, tells us that in 1944, when Korea was under severe and oppressive Japanese military rule, Soen-sa joined an underground independence movement and was caught, narrowly escaping death. After a prison sentence, he and two companions escaped to China, hoping to join the Free Korean Army.

They did not succeed, and after the war Soen-sa started university in South Korea, studying western philosophy. Time passed, and the situation in Korea grew steadily worse. One day Soen-sa decided that neither politics nor academic studies were ways in which he could be of use to people, and he left the university, shaved his head and went into the mountains, vowing never to return until he had found the absolute truth.

A monk in a small mountain temple introduced him to Buddhism by giving him the *Diamond Sutra* to read – that same sutra which had first enlightened Hui Neng. Soen-sa's mind became clear when he read the words, 'All things that appear in this world are transient. If you view all things that appear as never having appeared, then you will realize your true self.'

In 1948 he was ordained a Buddhist monk.

His understanding of the truth contained in the sutras needed practice to give him full realization, and so he began a hundred-day retreat on Won Gak, the Mountain of Perfect Enlightenment. A continuous diet of pine needles beaten into powder, combined with a daily number of ice-cold baths and twenty hours each day spent chanting, after a time produced some very strong doubts as to why he was going to such extremes. He thought enviously of Japanese Soto monks who live quietly and happily in small temples with their families, and find enlightenment gradually. These thoughts were so persuasive that one night he decided to leave and packed his things. But the next morning his will was strong again and he unpacked. During the following weeks he packed and unpacked nine times.

After a time he began to see visions, both terrible and beautiful. On the hundredth day, while he was sitting outside chanting and beating a moktak (a gong),

> his body disappeared and he was in infinite space. From far away he could hear the moktak beating, and the sound of his own voice. He remained in this state for some time. When he returned to his body, he understood. The rocks, the river, everything he could see, everything he could hear, all this was his true Self. All things are exactly as they are. The truth is just like this.

He came down from the mountain and went to the Zen Master Ko Bong, said to be the greatest in Korea and the hardest, for advice on how to practise.

Ko Bong said, 'A monk once asked Zen Master Jo-Ju, "Why did Bodhidharma come to China?" Jo-Ju answered, "The pine tree in the front garden." What does this mean?' Soen-sa understood the koan, but he didn't know how to answer. He said, 'I don't know.' Ko Bong said, 'Only keep this don't-know mind. That is true Zen practice.'

Throughout the summer Soen-sa worked out of doors. In the autumn he went to Su Dok Sa Monastery for a hundred-day meditation session. He learned the language of Zen verbal cross-fire and debate. In the winter he went a bit wild and played various tricks on the monks and nuns in that monastery to wake them up, but he was found out and made to apologize to everyone.

Then he went to Zen Master Chun Song, famous for his own wild actions, to test his satori. Soen-sa bowed to him and said, 'I killed all the Buddhas of past, present and future. What can you do?' Chun Song said 'Aha!' and looked deeply into Soen-sa's eyes. Then he asked, 'What did you see?' Soen-sa said, 'You already understand.' Chun Song said, 'Is that all?' Soen-sa said, 'There's a cuckoo singing in the tree outside the window.' Chun Song laughed and said, 'Aha!'. After several more questions, which Soen-sa answered easily, Chun Song delightedly shouted, 'You are enlightened! You are enlightened!'

When the hundred-day session was over, Soen-sa went to visit his first master, Ko Bong. On the way he twice more received inka, the seal of validation of his awakening, from the Zen Masters Keum Bong and Keum Oh.

When he arrived at Ko Bong's temple, Ko Bong questioned him on some of the most difficult of the 1,700 traditional koans. Soen-sa answered without hesitating. Then Ko Bong said, 'All right, one last question. The mouse eats cat-food, but the cat-bowl is broken. What does this mean?'·

Soen-sa answered, 'The sky is blue, the grass is green.'

Ko Bong shook his head and said, 'No.'

Soen-sa had never been wrong over a Zen question before and could not believe he had slipped up now. Every 'like-this' answer he gave was wrong, and Ko Bong kept shaking his head. At last Soen-sa shouted, 'Three Zen masters have given me inka. Why do you say I'm wrong?'

Ko Bong merely said, 'What does it mean? Tell me.'

After fifty minutes of absolute and intense silence, Soen-sa suddenly knew. The answer was 'Just like this.'

Joyfully Ko Bong embraced Soen-sa, saying, 'You are the flower and I am the bee.'

On 25 January 1949, Soen-sa received from Ko Bong his Transmission, thus becoming the Seventy-Eighth Patriarch in that particular line of succession. It was the only Transmission that Ko Bong ever gave.

After the ceremony, Ko Bong said to Soen-sa, 'For the next three years you must keep silent. You are a free man. We will meet again in five hundred years.'

Soen-sa was then a Zen master. He was twenty-two years old.

Korean Zen is considered closer to the original Chinese tradition than modern Japanese Zen. For instance it is not split into Rinzai and Soto sects, and most Korean monasteries include monks studying ways other than Zen. At most Korean monasteries the monks sit – many simply cross their legs rather than use the half or full lotus posture – for three months during the winter and summer sessions (from nine to thirteen hours a day, depending on the monastery) and for the other six months are free to wander or study at other temples. There is a formal speech by the master once or twice a month, but no such thing as regular interviews. If a monk feels he has reached some understanding, he goes to check with the master; otherwise, no reason. Individual long retreats are more common than in Japan; monks will go off to a hermitage for 100 or 1,000 days or five years, then return and present their understanding to the master. And before a student is given inka he must defeat (or at least strongly hold his ground with) three other Zen masters as well as his own.

Soen-sa uses a number of traditional koans from mainly Chinese and Korean sources; but he feels himself unattached to any form or tradition, Zen or otherwise. For instance he conducted a three-day session on Big Sur, California, giving his students eight hours a day of high-energy chanting, accompanied by drums, tambourines, skillets, moktaks, bells and other instruments. Thirty people banged away for hours, chanting at the top of their lungs. This was Soen-sa's invention, designed for Californian karma; and many people who could never sit Zen, or who had been doing sesshins (Zen sessions) for years without the slightest experience of real clarity, were able to drink deeply of the joy and power of One Mind.

Soen-sa uses much mantra chanting in his practice, especially for students who find the koan 'What am I?' or breath meditation extremely difficult. Usually these are intellectuals with constantly churning minds (especially psychologists and philosophers) or people (most often women) with very strong emotions. But in the end mantra meditation is thought to be no different from koan meditation or shikan-taza. The techniques are different, but the don't-know mind that they lead to is the same. Each technique is like a river bank: one stands there and watches the river flow without tumbling in and being carried off by the current: until there is nothing to stand on and no one to stand.

But the main emphasis of Soen-sa's teaching is on keeping a clear mind during the entire course of one's day: 'Everyday mind is the path.' He has found that many students who have been practising Japanese Zen become tremendously attached to sitting, and hence create a distinction between meditation and other activities. So, although his close students have a solid sitting practice, he will usually teach that techniques and body sitting are not important: what is important is how you are keeping your mind at this very moment.

A Bodhisattva, having renounced the final state of Nirvana in order to help all sentient beings to attain liberation, is the ideal of the Mahayana school of Buddhism, to which Zen belongs. He is often called a Buddha of compassion, as purposeless and effortless love in action is his aim. Sattva – Being or Essence – is Bodhi, the Wisdom that arises from direct perception of the truth. The 'pensive' posture, seen here, is said to be that of reflective contemplation. (Bodhisattva Miroku, a Future Buddha, seated figure, Japan, 7th c.)

The lotus is the Buddhist symbol of enlightenment, for the roots are embedded in the mud (of human passions) while the leaf and flower open up to the sun (in purity). (Lotus leaf at Ryoanji Zen Monastery, Kyoto, Japan.)

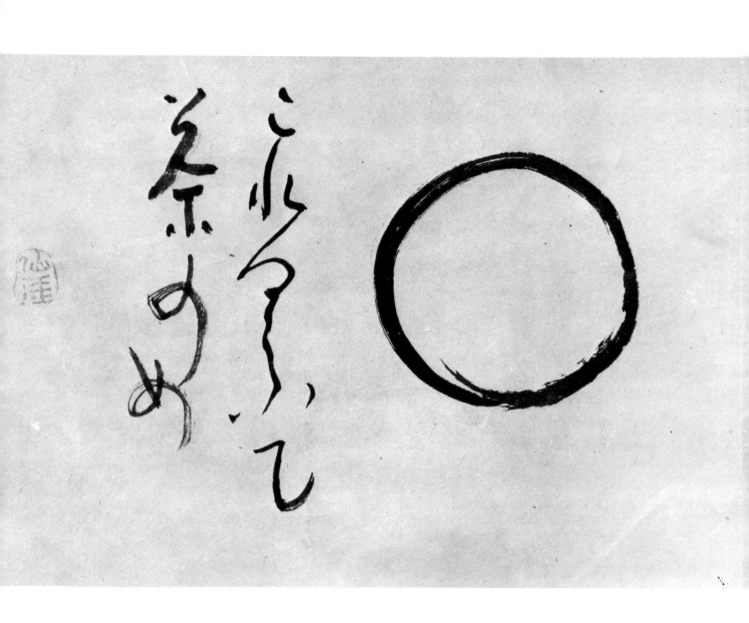

The circle represents on one level
the totality of the universe and on
another level its ultimate voidness.
(Circle, ink drawing by Zen Master
Sengai, Japan, 18th c.)

乳竇秋高樹憑虛一小亭倚身還怯已登岑且停已憩意盡歸此開情隔浦汀溪山如好舊一醉十年醒　重登水西　清湘老人

Once more climbing Shui-hsi

In the jumbled valleys high autumn
    trees,
Ascending the void, one small shel-
    ter.
I stop to rest, then hasten on again,
I climb on foot, yet continually halt.

The lonesome feeling here returns
    complete;
My idle thoughts are far from the
    river bank.
Brook and hill are like good old
    friends,
Once drunk, and ten years to wake.

(Leaf from Views of the South, writ-
ten and painted by Tao Chi, a
Ch'an/Zen monk whose monastic
name was Bitter Melon, China, 17th
c. Translation by Roderick
Whitfield.)

The great formative age of the Ch'an (Zen) calligraphic style was the Sung Dynasty (AD 959–1279). The Sung masters were pre-eminently landscape painters, creators of mountain, mist, rock and tree paintings that have never been surpassed. They portray a world which is complete in itself, having no motive or purpose other than being just what it is. (Haze dispersing from around a mountain town, one of the Eight Views of the Hsiao Hsiang, ink painting, China, 13th c.)

A Zen student monk at a temple in Japan. He is meditating on things as they are, allowing them to pass through the mind without leaving a trace. (Photo by Takamasa Inamura.)

Since Zen meditation is a way of realizing oneness with the world, and is not an escape from it, the eyes of Zen monks are never quite closed. (Monk contemplating the monastery garden at Daitokuji Zen Temple, Kyoto, Japan, photo by Roloff Beny.)

The peach offered by the monkey symbolizes, among other things, sexual enjoyment, and the sage contemplates this temptation which, like all thoughts, will emerge and die within his mind. The painting is on a leaf of the pippala, which is believed to be the Bodhi (Wisdom) tree beneath which the Buddha came to his enlightenment. (A monkey offers a peach to a sage, from album of Buddhist ascetics, China, 19th c.)

40

Meditating in a landscape. (Painting
attributed to the Ch'an/Zen monk
Fan-lung, China, 12th c.)

Before studying Zen, says a famous Zen maxim, one sees mountains as mountains and waters as waters. When one reaches a more intimate knowledge one sees that mountains are not mountains and waters are not waters. But when one reaches the very substance one is at rest. For then one sees mountains once again as mountains and waters once again as waters. (Japanese Zen monks at a waterfall.)

平沙煙
樹遠模
糊雲鎖
青山半
有無行
佛王維
筆瑞畫
出軸此
蓋舊時畫
蔬菜莢寒云
及此箒閒
此幅似道大
年之本牌
縣没肖商
未沉劃題

曉烟吹凍
有無間着煙
詩翁者好山
看到山堂煙
滿處笑寒衣

題
申繹步

如坡公以云
空濛年歷烟
而出沒時也
朗霽清粗不
減怨先對子
范々我六宇
人臣卫
右人見
之又張
學我
悔蕃個

澹若
無筆
我學去

題
雁園倪篆

法富有幹遠之鑰
王程

鉅鹿楊鬼聖

意想所佶一空
諸相竹其今我
儘也為

The Ch'an (Zen) artist Hu Yu K'un balances form with emptiness, but an emptiness which is intrinsic to the painting and is not merely un-filled background. (Landscape by Hu Yu K'un, China, 17th c.)

Hui Neng, the Sixth Patriarch of Ch'an (Zen) Buddhism and one of the earliest Zen Masters, is here portrayed in a Sung Dynasty mural. He said: 'The capacity of the mind is as great as that of space. It is infinite, neither round nor square, neither great nor small, neither right nor wrong, neither good nor evil. Intrinsically, our transcendental nature is empty, and not a single thing can be attained. It is the same with the essence of mind, which is a state of absolute void.' (Hui Neng, painting, China, 10th–13th c.)

Such a painting as this exemplifies the Ch'an (Zen) style in which form seems to float in space as the objects of the world come into, and disappear within, the emptiness of the mind. A temple roof can be seen as an intrinsic part of the landscape. (Misty landscape, painting attributed to Mi Fei, China, ?10th–13th c.)

The Japanese Zen monk Sesshu was a master of powerful, rough brush strokes. Rocks and bamboo are sharply actual against the background of mountain and space, as though experienced for the first time. The actuality of the living, immediate present is one of the forms taken by Zen realization. (Landscape in Haboku style, painting by Sesshu, Japan, 1495.)

Zen monasteries, their roots in Buddhism, display many representations of the Arhats, the enlightened disciples of the Buddha. (The Rakan Binzuru or Arhat Pindala, seated figure, Japan, 13th c.)

The uncomplicated harmony between human beings and nature is a characteristic preoccupation of Zen artists. Here the figures are in motion between the still cliff and the turbulent water. (The Red Cliff on the Yangtse, painting by Li Sung, China, 10th–13th c.)

In Kendo two swordsmen face each other in a meditation of oneness with action. 'Do' means way, or teaching method, and Kendo is the way of swordsmanship. Meditation does not always imply quietude or physical stillness. In Kendo the meditative state is one of absolute attentiveness and control. The mind is immovable, however much the body is moving to meet changing circumstances.

Still activity (left) is intense
concentration in which
identification takes place between
the person and his behaviour;
active stillness (above) is a
concentrated awareness in which
the mind is as taut as a stretched
bowstring. The monk is as alert as
the swordsman. (Monk
contemplating the Great Sea
Garden of Daisen-in at Daitokuji
Zen Monastery, Kyoto, Japan.)

A scene of monastic life in a Zen community: the abbot reads a letter aloud to his monks. (Painting of the Tosa school, Japan, 17th c.)

Monks in zazen, the practice of
sitting meditation. In Soto Zen the
monks face outwards, gazing at the
wall; in Rinzai Zen they face in-
wards. In this seated position the
body becomes like a rock, and the
mind gains the strength of immova-
bility beneath the ever-changing
flow of thoughts.

A realization of the Chinese character for 'man'. (Calligraphy by Jiun, Japan, 18th c.)

Chinese characters lend themselves to a style which is a blend of painting and writing. Chinese black ink is capable of a variety of tones, depending on the admixture of water, and the solid stick of ink itself is found in a number of qualities and shades of black. Writing is done with a sharply pointed brush set in a bamboo stem. The touch must be light and fluid and continuous if the ink is to flow regularly, and so its control requires free movements of hand and arm, a freedom which is the result of inner certainty and understanding. Consequently one brush stroke can tell a master the extent of his pupil's liberation. (Sanskrit calligraphy by Zen Master Hakuin, Japan, 18th c.)

The Buddha's disciple Wu Liang-shan. (Painting by Li Ken, China, 18th c.)

A phantom Samurai descends in wrath: a scene close to Noh drama. The Samurai military caste of Japan adopted the principles of Zen as the most effective religious way of dealing with the pressing problem of life and death. The Kamakura era (the thirteenth century) was the one in which Zen became firmly established as a warrior religion. At that time the spirit of Japan lay in its priesthood and its soldiery, and the spiritual blending of these two professions created 'the way of the warrior'. (Phantom warrior, painting of Tosa School, Japan, 17th c.)

There is a story that Master Lin-chi (Rinzai) was once planting pine trees when along came his master, Huang Po (Obaku), who asked him, 'Why are you planting so many pines in this remote mountain monastery?' Rinzai answered, 'They will look nice around the monastery gate and they will benefit those who come after us.' Then he struck the ground three times with his hoe. Huang Po said, 'Though this may be so, yet I'll give you thirty blows with my stick.' Again Rinzai struck the ground three times with his hoe, while he sighed deeply. Huang Po said, 'Through you our school will flourish throughout the world.' (Zen Masters Tokusan, on the left, and Rinzai, right and below, triptych by Zen Master Sengai, Japan, 18th c.)

Bodhidarma (known in Japan as Daruma) is the semi-legendary First Patriarch of Zen, who came to China from India in the sixth century AD. Traditionally he had a fierce gaze and was uncompromising in his teaching. It is related in China that he sat facing a wall for nine years in meditation. Finding himself constantly overcome by sleep, he pulled off his eyelashes and threw them to the ground, where they sprang up as the first tea plants. Monks afterwards used less drastic means for keeping awake! (Daruma, painting after Jakuchu, Japan, 18th c.)

The second disciple of the Buddha, who created a pearly palace from a vase simply by snapping his fingers. The palace symbolizes Nirvana, and thus the whole picture indicates the rapidity with which he reached enlightenment. Another image from the same series is reproduced on the cover of this book. (Image from ms. on the Eighteen Lohans or Disciples of the Buddha, China, 19th c.)

Buddhist disciple playing with cymbals. (Painting on a pippala leaf, China, 19th c.)

Yuima, whose Indian name was Vimalakirti, is the principal figure of a famous Buddhist scripture, the *Vimalakirti Sutra*. He is said to have been a wealthy householder in the time of the Buddha. He was a great philanthropist and a philosopher, highly learned in the scriptures. So sharp was his understanding that it is said that, when he was ill and the Buddha wanted to send one of his disciples to him, each one refused to go on the grounds that no one was equal to the task of talking to the great philosopher-saint. All had been worsted by him in debate on previous occasions. (Yuima, painting by Ogata Korin, Zen artist of Edo period, Japan, 17th–18th c.)

Hui Neng, the Sixth Patriarch of Zen, is here seen tearing up the scriptures to show his uncompromising preference for personal, first-hand experience as against the words of others, as well as his abhorrence of too reverent an attitude to supposedly holy subjects. One of his successors, Lin-chi (Rinzai), expressed the same attitude in the words, 'If the Buddha blocks your way to the truth, kill him!' (Hui Neng, painting by Liang K'ai, China, c.1200.)

The empty courtyard of a Zen temple. Inner space merges into outer, so that outside and inside become one.

Themes

A seated sage. A few vigorous brush strokes bring the whole of Zen to life. Form is balanced with emptiness and painting is created by not-painting. (Drawing by Boshodo, Japan. British Museum, London.)

A Conversation with Master Seung Sahn

What is Zen?

What are you?

(Silence.)

Do you understand?

I don't know.

This don't-know mind is you. Zen is understanding yourself.

Is that all Zen is?

Isn't it enough?

I mean, there must be a final understanding or illumination that a Zen master has in order to be a Zen master.

All understanding is no understanding. What do *you* understand? Show me!

(Silence.)

Okay, what is one plus two?

Three.

Why didn't you tell me *that*? What colour is the sky?

Blue.

Very good! The truth is very simple, yah? But your mind is complicated; you understand too much. So you could not answer. But you don't understand one thing.

What?

One plus two equals zero.

I don't see how.

Okay. Suppose someone gives me an apple. I eat it. Then he gives me two more apples. I eat them. All the apples are gone. So one plus two equals zero.

Hmmm.

You must understand this. Before you were born, you were zero. Now you are one. In the future, you will die and again become zero. All things in the universe are like this; they arise from emptiness and return to emptiness. So zero equals one, one equals zero.

I see that.

In elementary school, they teach that one plus two equals three. In our Zen elementary school, we teach that one plus two equals zero. Which one is correct?

Both.

If you say 'both', I say 'neither'.

Why?

If you say 'both', then the space ship cannot go to the moon. When only one plus two equals three, then it can reach the moon. But if one plus two also equals zero, then on the way the space ship will disappear. So I say, neither is correct.

Then what would be a proper answer?

'Both' is wrong, so I hit you. Also 'neither' is wrong, so I hit myself. The first teaching in Buddhism is 'form is emptiness, emptiness is form.' This means that one equals zero, zero equals one. But who makes form? Who makes emptiness? Both form and emptiness are concepts. Concepts are made by your own thinking.

Descartes said, 'I think, therefore I am.' But if I am not thinking, then what? Before thinking, there is no you or I, no form or emptiness, no right or wrong. So even 'no form, no emptiness' is wrong. In true emptiness, before thinking, you only keep a clear mind. All things are just as they are. 'Form is form, emptiness is emptiness.'

I'm afraid I still don't really understand.

If you *want* to understand, already this is a mistake. Only go straight ahead and keep don't-know mind. Then you will understand everything.

What is enlightenment?

Enlightenment is only a name. If you *make* enlightenment, then enlightenment exists. But if enlightenment exists, ignorance exists too. Good and bad, right and wrong, enlightened and ignorant – all these are opposites. All opposites are just your own thinking. The truth is absolute, beyond thinking, beyond opposites. If you make something, you will get something. But if you don't make anything, you will get everything.

Is enlightenment really just a name? Doesn't a Zen master have to attain the experience of enlightenment in order to be a Zen master?

The Heart Sutra says that there is no attainment, with nothing to attain. If enlightenment is attained, it is not enlightenment.

Then is everyone enlightened?

Do you understand no-attainment?

No.

No-attainment is attainment. You must attain no-attainment! So what is attainment? What is there to attain?

Emptiness?

In true emptiness, there is no name and no form. So there is no attainment. If you say 'I have attained true emptiness', you are wrong.

I'm beginning to understand. That is, I think I am.

The universe is always true emptiness. Now you are living in a dream. Wake up! Then you will understand.

How can I wake up?

I hit you! Very easy.

Would you please explain a bit more?

Okay. Can you see your eyes?

In a mirror.

That is not your eyes: it is only their reflection. Your eyes cannot see themselves. If you want to see your eyes, there is already a mistake. If you want to understand your mind, there is already a mistake.

But when you were a young monk, you had the actual experience of enlightenment. What was this experience?

I hit you.

(Silence.)

Okay, suppose we have before us some honey, some sugar, and a banana. All are sweet. Can you explain the difference between honey's sweetness, sugar's sweetness, and banana's sweetness?

Hmmm.

But each is a different sweetness, yah? How can you explain to me?

I don't know.

But you could say, 'Open your mouth. *This* is honey, *this* is sugar, *this* is banana.' So to understand your true self, you must understand the meaning of my hitting you. I have already put enlightenment into your mind.

You mentioned 'clear mind'. What is that?

We can talk about three separate minds. The first is attachment mind. This is called losing your mind. Next is keeping one mind. The third is clear mind. For example, you are standing in a train station and suddenly there is a loud whistle blast. You are startled out of yourself: no self, no world, only the whistle. Or if you haven't eaten for three days and someone gives you food, you gobble it down without thinking. There is only the eating. Or when you are having sex, there is only the good feeling, the absorption in the other person. This is losing your mind. But afterwards, when you stop having sex, your small, selfish mind is just as strong as ever. These are attachment actions. They come from desire and end in suffering.

What is keeping one mind?

When someone is reciting a mantra, there is only the mantra. He sees good, and there is only 'Om mani padme hum'. He sees bad, and there is only 'Om mani padme hum'. Whatever he does, whatever he sees, there is only the mantra.

Then what is clear mind?

Clear mind is like a mirror. Red comes, and the mirror is red; white comes, and the mirror is white. When all people are sad, I am sad; when all people are happy, I am happy. If your mind is without any attachments at all, if you have no desires for yourself, but only want to help all people, that is clear mind. So the mind that is lost in desire is small mind. One mind is empty mind. Clear mind is big mind, which is infinite time and infinite space.

It's still not completely clear to me. Could you give another example, please?

Okay. Suppose a man and a woman are having sex. They have lost their minds and are very very happy. Just then, a robber breaks in with a gun and says, 'Give me your money!' All their happiness disappears and they are very scared. 'Oh help me, help me!' This is small mind. It is constantly changing, as outside conditions change.

Next, someone is doing mantra. His mind is not moving at all. There is no inside or outside, only true emptiness. The robber appears. 'Give me money!' But the person is not afraid. Only 'Om mani padme hum. Om mani padme hum.' 'Give me money or I'll kill you!' He doesn't care. Already there is no life and no death. So he is not in the least afraid.

Next is clear mind. This person always keeps the great mirror mind of true compassion. The robber appears. 'Give me money!' This person says, 'How much do you want?' 'Give me everything!' 'Okay' – and he gives the robber all his money. He is not afraid. But his mind is very sad. He is thinking, 'Why are you doing this? Now you are all right, but in the future you will have much suffering.' The robber looks at him and sees that he is not afraid, that there is only motherly compassion on his face. So the robber is a little confused. The person is already teaching him the correct way, and maybe some day, many years from now, he will remember and be able to hear.

Clear mind is the mind of absolute love. It is perfect freedom. If you have selfish desires, your love is not true love. It is dependent on many conditions; if these change, you suffer. Suppose you love a woman very much, and she loves you. You go away on a trip, and when you return you find that she has taken another lover. Your love changes to anger and hatred. So small love always contains the seeds of suffering. Big love has no suffering. It is *only* love, so it is beyond joy and beyond suffering.

What do you do with your freedom?

When I am hungry, I eat. When I am tired, I sleep.

What kind of formal practice would you recommend to beginners? I know that at your Zen Centers in America, your students do sitting meditation for several hours each day. Is that necessary?

Meditation is important. But what is most important is how you keep your mind, just now, from moment to moment to moment. Body sitting is not necessary; it is only one kind of outside form. What is necessary is mind sitting. True sitting means cutting off all thinking and keeping a mind that doesn't move. True Zen means becoming clear. When I asked you 'What are you?' you didn't know. There was only don't-know. If you keep this don't-know mind when you are driving, this is driving Zen. If you keep it when you are playing tennis, this is tennis Zen. If you keep it when you are watching television, this is television Zen. You must keep don't-know mind always and everywhere. This is the true practice of Zen. 'The Great Way is not difficult: just don't be attached to distinctions. If you can let go of your own likes and dislikes, then everything will become perfectly clear.'

Is it important to have a teacher?

Very important! Many people practise on their own and come to think that they understand. They think that they are great enlightened Bodhisattvas. But that is only their own thinking. So it is necessary to visit a great Zen master

Paintings of Dogen (see p. 19) are rare; this one shows a calm and reflective aspect. (Zen Master Dogen, self-portrait, Japan, 13th c.)

Sengai calls his black-and white portrait of Lin-chi (Rinzai, see p. 16) 'The fist that strikes the teacher'. (Rinzai, portrait by Zen Master Sengai, Japan, 18th c.)

Hakuin (see p. 22), who painted himself in many different styles, here sits with a hosshu (flywhisk of horsehair) in his hand. Zen Master Hakuin, self-portrait, Japan, 18th c. Eisei Bunko.)

and win his approval. Otherwise the blind will be leading the blind, and everyone will fall into a ditch.

In the Zen school, we have many kong-ans [koans]. Kong-ans are like tests. Or like fishing hooks. If your mind is not clear, the baited hook will drop into the pool of your mind and all your thinking will appear. And you will touch the hook and be caught. But if you have attained true enlightenment, seventeen hundred hooks can go into your mind and you will have no hindrance. The hook drops into clear water and comes out of clear water. No fish.

But what if someone can't find a Zen master?
Then they can always write to me.
Are there any kong-ans they could try to answer, to test their minds?
Well, the first two kong-ans in our school are ones they might try.

A. Buddha said that all things have Buddha-nature. But when someone asked Zen Master Jo-ju if a dog has Buddha-nature, he said 'Mu' ('No'). I have three questions:

1) Buddha said yes, Jo-ju said no. Which one is correct?

2) Jo-ju said, 'Mu'. What does this mean?

3) I ask you, does a dog have Buddha-nature?

B. A monk once said to Jo-ju, 'I have just arrived at your temple. Please teach me.' Jo-ju said, 'Have you had breakfast?' The monk said, 'Yes.' Jo-ju said, 'Then go wash your bowls'. The monk was suddenly enlightened. My question is, what did this monk attain?

If you *want* to understand the answers to these kong-ans, you will never never understand. But if you only go straight ahead and keep don't-know mind, then the answers will appear by themselves. And when your mind becomes completely clear, you will be able to answer any kong-an without hindrance.

Thank you very much.
You're welcome.

Hakuin here caricatures himself as Pu-tei (Hotei, see p. 89), the god of good fortune, supporting his generous belly as he meditates. (Zen Master Hakuin, self-portrait, Japan, 18th c. Eisei Bunko.)

The nun Shido in meditation, her shoes beneath her seat. Shido founded the Zen Temple of Tokei-ji in Japan. (Shido, seated figure, Japan, 14 c.)

Master Seung Sahn (see pp. 66–67). The dialogue between Master Seung Sahn and a student, printed here, was supplied to the author especially for inclusion in this book.

Zen Master Shunryu Suzuki (see p. 26).

The Bodhisattva ideal, that of the saviour of the world who vows not to enter Nirvana but to be born again and again until even the grass and the dust attain Buddhahood, is implicit in Zen. (Bodhisattva, painting by Cho Cho, China, 10th c. Museum für chinesische Kunst, Staatliche Museen Preussischer Kulturbesitz, West Berlin.)

Sanzen: a master in private interview with a student. On these occasions the student is expected to bring forth, perhaps wordlessly, all that he has discovered since the last interview. The master may reply with a grunt, a warm smile, or a question which shows the student another aspect of his koan.

The Buddha in the mudra or attitude of teaching. (Buddha of the Western Paradise, Japan, 13th c. Victoria and Albert Museum, London.)

A Zen abbot delivers his lecture, or Dharma talk. 'Taking the high seat' is a well-known Zen term for the master in his chair. (Photo by Horace Bristol.)

When the Buddha preached for the first time after his enlightenment, he imparted the doctrine called the Wheel of the Law. This mudra (gesture) recalls the Wheel, or the teaching of the doctrine, and it is thus a teaching mudra. The circle formed by thumb and index finger is complete, having neither beginning nor end. It is perfection, as is the Buddha's law, which is perfect and eternal. (Detail of Buddha figure, Yakushi-ji Temple,

Meditation

A Zen monk meditating in the mountains. (Painting attributed to Jonin, Japan, 13th c. Kozan-ji, Tokyo.)

The frog has been a popular subject for Zen artists, since, like a good meditator, it remains for hours in a motionless position but without ever losing awareness of life around it. (Meditating frog, painting by Zen Master Sengai, Japan, 18th c. Idemitsu Art Gallery, Tokyo.)

Zazen: meditation in a nuns' Soto Zendo (meditation hall) in Japan. The head nun holds up her keisaku, the stick with which she will whack the shoulders of any nun who bows her head as a signal that it is needed to correct dozing or daydreaming. (Photo by Nakada.)

Rinzai monks in zazen on a raised platform (*tan*) 8 feet wide and 3 feet high. The centre floor is used for *kinhin*, a periodic walking in single file along the *tan*, which is practised to prevent the monks' minds from falling into torpor. Zazen has two aspects: one is *shi* (stopping) and the other is

kan (view). By sitting, the moving, wavering, everyday mind is quieted and a calm and clear mind able to see the reality of things takes its place. This is *shi*; by the presence of *shi* an objective view of the world in which everything is seen as it is, arises, and this is *kan*. (Photo by Takamasa Inamura.)

Monks in meditation. (Caricature by Gien Soto, Japan, 20th c. Institute of Zen Studies, Kyoto.)

Landscape

Tree, mountain, man and space blend into one. (Landscape with Figures, painting attributed to Emperor Hui-tsung, China, 12th c. Konchi-in, Kyoto.)

The principle of *li* (innermost reality) in Zen painting is shown perfectly in this tranquil scene. *Li* transcends form and yet is inherent in every atom. Every painter must identify himself with the *li* (or Suchness) of what he paints so that the painting reveals the *li* of its subject. He must do this by sacrificing his own ego, for the perception of *li* can only occur when 'I–my–me' is out of the way. A painting which is not based on the intuitive apprehension of the *li* of its subject is not considered worthy of true art, no matter how carefully and faithfully the picture might reflect external shapes and colours. (Boating by Moonlight, painting attributed to Ma Yüan, China, 13th c. British Museum, London.)

In contrast to Ma Yüan's moonlight boating scene, this painting by a Japanese Zen artist takes us right into the *li* of storm, with waves rising and the wind twisting the jagged branches of a tree. (Landscape and Boat in Stormy Weather, painting by Shukei Sesson, Japan, 16th c. Bunei Nomura Collection.)

Tung-shan was a ninth-century Chinese master. One day when he was crossing a stream he saw his own reflection in it. He at once composed the following poem:

Do not seek the truth from others:
Further and further he will retreat from
    you.
Alone I now go,
And I come across him wherever
    I look.
He is no other than myself,
And yet I am not he.
When this is understood,
I am face to face with Tathata
    [Suchness].

(Tung-shan Crossing the Stream, painting by Ma Yüan, China, 13th c. National Museum, Tokyo.)

Trying to Catch a Catfish with a Gourd, by Josetsu, a noted Zen painter. (Painting by Josetsu, Japan, 15th c. Taizo-in, Myoshin-ji, Kyoto.)

Landscape

A famous Zen painter, K'un-ts'an, said: 'Speaking of painting in its finest essentials, one must read widely in the documents and the histories, ascend mountains, and trace rivers to their sources, and only then can one create one's ideas.' (Clear Weather in the Valley, painting formerly attributed to Tung Yüan, China, 11th–13th c. Courtesy Museum of Fine Arts, Boston. Chinese and Japanese Special Fund.)

The innate rhythm of sky, mountains, tree and temple reveals the *li* of landscape. A Chinese poet, Wang-wei, said:
In the empty hills just after rain,
The evening air is autumn now.
(Clearing Autumn Skies over Mountains and Valleys, painting attributed to Kuo Hsi, China, 11th c. Courtesy of the Smithsonian Institution, Freer Gallery of Art, Washington DC.)

Great space accentuates the sharp mountain peaks, which themselves float in mist; and yet every leaf is evident in the tree which dominates the foreground. Such is the make-up of Zen, the infinite and the immediate merged into one. (Houses on a Lake, painting attributed to Shubun, Japan, 16th c. Courtesy Museum of Fine Arts, Boston. Bigelow Collection.)

The garden

The earliest landscape gardens in Japanese monasteries and temples were laid out soon after the introduction of Buddhism from Korea in the sixth century. The aim was to 'capture alive' the beauty of natural scenery. When Zen became popular in the twelfth century the simplicity of such gardens became so extreme, mainly composed as they were of white sand, rocks and moss, that they could be appreciated only by those who had some measure of Zen understanding. The aim of a Zen garden is to bring alive in the spectator the meaning of the hidden essentials behind outward appearances. The dry landscape (as shown below left) is a favourite Zen style, because space is used in a pure and symbolic way, while a meticulous pattern of ridges, in perfect proportion to its area, is made on the level, white sea-sand by a bamboo rake.

A Buddha statue in the attitude of supreme enlightenment sits among the leaves and flowers of the Ryoan-ji Zen Monastery garden in Kyoto.

A stone causes a ripple in the Totekiko stone garden, demonstrating the truth that the still water (mind) reflects reality purely, but as soon as a stone (thought) makes ripples reality becomes distorted. (Ryogen-in Zen Monastery garden, Kyoto.)

Patterns in white sand. (Ryogen-in and Zaiko-in Zen Monastery gardens, Kyoto.)

Zen in action

Monks exercising on Mount Hiei at dawn.

Zen monk filling an urn with water. (Photo by Horace Bristol.)

A monk strikes the Ogane, the largest bell in the monastery, with the heavy swinging beam. This bell reflects the spirit of the temple and has a particularly mind-pacifying effect. (Matsushima Zen Monastery, Japan. Photo by Horace Bristol.)

Zen monks gardening (Caricature by Gien Soto, Japan, 20th c. Institute of Zen Studies, Kyoto.)

A monk strikes the great wooden fish. The inside is hollow and when it is beaten with a padded stick the sound produced is said to have a hypnotic effect on the hearer. When used to accompany sutra-readings it brings the minds of the audience to a properly receptive state.

Monks having their heads shaved. (Photo by Takamasa Inamura.)

A Zen monk uses a block of ink, water and a brush to write short sutras, scriptural texts, on strips of wood. (Photo by Horace Bristol.)

The Blue-countenanced Bearer of the Thunderbolt. (Calligraphy by Zen Master Hakuin, Japan, 18th c. Private collection.)

82

Haiku is a particularly Zen form of poetry; for Zen detests egoism in the form of calculated effects or self-glorification of any sort. The author of haiku should be absent, and only the haiku present, so that there can be no artifice or ulterior motive. It consists of seventeen syllables into which is put the most sublime feeling that human beings are capable of. 'A haiku is the expression of a temporary enlightenment in which we see into the life of things' (R. H. Blyth). In Buddhist terms it expresses the Suchness of each thing. Basho (seventeenth century) is one of the most famous haiku poets. His enlightenment came when he heard the sound of the water as a frog jumped into a pond, and he wrote:

The still pond, ah!
A frog jumps in:
The water's sound!

(Haiku poets of the school of Basho, painting by Buson, Japan, 1828. British Museum, London.)

Hakuin appended to this painting of a monkey a verse which says:

The monkey is reaching for the moon
  in the water,
Until death overtakes him he will never
  give up.
If he would only let go the branch and
  disappear into the deep pool,
The whole world would shine with
  dazzling clearness.

(Monkey, painting by Zen Master Hakuin, Japan, 18th c. Eisei Bunko.)

Humour

A renowned Buddhist student of the 4th century AD retired to Lu-shan and was a hermit for thirty years. When he saw his visitors off, he never went beyond the mountain stream called Hu (tiger). One day two visitors, a great poet and a Taoist, called on him. They became so interested in their talk that the hermit forgot all about the bridge and walked beyond it. Suddenly a tiger roared loudly. They looked at each other and laughed heartily before they parted. Later, a pavilion was built there, dedicated to the Three Laughing Ones. (Three Sages Laughing on Rohan Bridge, painting by Soga Shohaku, Japan. Courtesy Museum of Fine Arts, Boston, Bigelow Collection.)

The story goes that Tan-Hsia, a wandering Ch'an (Zen) monk of the thirteenth century, came to an old deserted temple one cold winter's night. The wind was piercing and the snow falling. Deciding that the best service the Buddha could perform would be to give him warmth, he burnt a wooden temple Buddha. (Tan-Hsia Burning the Buddha Image, painting by Zen Master Sengai, Japan, 18th c. Idemitsu Art Gallery, Tokyo.)

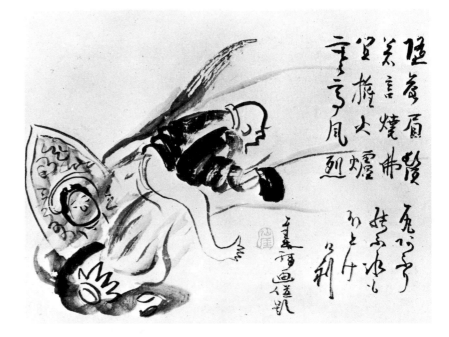

Han-shan and Shih-te, lunatic monks of the Tang Dynasty, were boon companions. Zen artists had a special fondness for painting them in their simplicity and spontaneous merriment. (Kanzan and Zittoku, or Han-shan and Shih-te, painting by Shubun, Japan, 15th c. National Museum, Tokyo.)

Kanzan (Han-shan) was a happy lunatic monk of the Tang Dynasty, who was also a renowned Ch'an (Zen) poet. Such black and white ink drawings, done with a few brush strokes or light touches of ink on a white ground, represent a particular way of Zen painting, a technique known as the 'thrifty brush' and the 'frugality of ink'. In order to express the natural Suchness of all things, the painter dispensed with everything unnecessary and used as few brush strokes and as little ink as possible. (Kanzan or Han-shan, painting by Kao, Japan, 14th c. Shoji Hattori Collection.)

Humour

It is characteristic of much Zen art to portray the sages in undignified attitudes: for misplaced reverence distracts from the true way. (Lohan Cleaning his Ear, painting by Ch'i-ch'eng, Japan. British Museum, London.)

Hsien-tzu or Kenzo was a Ch'an (Zen) devotee of great insight, who earned his livelihood, like any ordinary person, catching river fish. He had no home or possessions and usually slept in a shrine under the paper money offered to the god by the villagers. Zen Master Ching happened to hear of him and wanting to test Kenzo's understanding, hid himself under the paper money. At midnight he jumped out at the old fisherman as he came back, and asked, 'Why did the First Patriarch come to this country?' Without hesitation, Kenzo answered, 'The wine-stand in front of the god.' A later Zen master remarked, 'If it were not for this "wine-stand in front of the god", he would be merely a ghostly spirit.' (Kenzo Catching Prawns, painting by Kao, Japan, 14th c. National Museum, Tokyo.)

A Zen artist here deliberately reminds us that the Sixth Patriarch was a kitchen boy and wood-chopper. (Hui Neng Chopping Bamboo, painting by Ryankai, Japan, 13th c. National Museum, Tokyo.)

In a narrative scroll, Toba Sojo depicts a number of spirited and wittily observed animals frolicking at a picnic. Such scrolls are believed to be a satire on the behaviour of human beings, particularly the members of the upper classes. (Part of the Animal Scrolls attributed to Zen Abbot Toba Sojo, Japan, 12th c. Kozan-ji, Kyoto.)

主丈横桃会垂
臚脊魁瞽祐云
八尺荊棘園錄
凰家汲酒窝干
古萬真咸猶蹯
大川　　永賢

Humour

Pu-tei (Japanese Hotei), the greatbellied god of good fortune, with his sack of gifts on a pole over his shoulder, dances through the country. Pu-tei was a favourite subject for Zen artists, as he represents the spontaneously happy way in which the gods are supposed to have lived before the coming of mankind. (Pu-tei Dancing, painting by Liang K'ai, China, 13th c. Private Collection.)

Right-hand page
A master leans on a tiger. The tiger often symbolizes a fierce master; this one, and the master himself, seem momentarily somnolent. (Ch'an/Zen Monk in Meditation, painting by Shih-k'o, China, 10th c. National Museum, Tokyo.)

In this portrait of a Ch'an (Zen) priest the exaggerated and humorous emphasis on the belly, and the squat, square shape of the figure, reflect the 'settling into the self' of good Zen practice. (Ink Portrait of a Priest, painting by Liang K'ai, China, 13th c. National Palace Museum, Taipei.)

Daruma (Bodhidharma). Note the strength of the brush strokes which reflect wittily yet sympathetically on the fierce integrity of the subject. (Daruma, painting by Shokada, Japan, 17th c. R. G. Sawyers Collection.)

Martial arts

All martial arts are life-and-death struggles with one's own ego. They can be used for self-defence, but their real aim is self-knowledge, leading to Realization. In the way of archery the student must cultivate an inner balance of mind and outer mastery of the body so total that all movements arise without the intervention of thought; to take conscious aim is to deny this principle. When archery is performed in a state of 'no-thought' (*mushin*), which means the absence of *all* ego-consciousness, the archer is free from inhibitions as he puts an arrow to his bow, stretches the string, lets his eye rest on the target and, when the adjustment is correct, lets the arrow go. There is no feeling of good or bad, accomplishment or failure. This is the 'everyday mind' arising from 'no-mind', and it is the essence of all the Zen martial arts to remain in this state, with no thought of life or death.

When fear of injury or death affects the swordsman, his mind loses the fluidity of non-attachment. He must pass beyond his concepts of life and death and then his mind will follow its own course like water, and he will hold his sword as if not holding it.

Karate practice: the karate student must concentrate on using the most effective part of his body (frequently the hand) to attack the nerve centres of his opponent's body. His movements may follow a circular path or go in a straight line, according to which school he belongs to.

Zen archery, before and after: always an expression of immovable mind. The third-century Chinese sage Chuang Tzu records this story:
Lieh-tzu was exhibiting his archery to Po-hun Wu-jen. When his bow was fully stretched, a cup of water was placed on his elbow and he let fly. No sooner was the first arrow gone than a second was on the string, followed by a third, while all the time he stood motionless, like a statue. But Po-hun Wu-jen said, 'Your technique is fine, but it is not the shooting of non-shooting. Come, let's climb a high mountain, clambering over the great rocks to the edge of an eight-hundred-foot precipice – and then we'll see what kind of archery you'll do.'

They climbed a high mountain and stood on the edge of the precipice. Turning his back to the chasm, Po-hun Wu-jen stepped backwards until his feet hung over the edge by one half. Then he bowed to Lieh-tzu and asked him to come forward and join him. But Lieh-tzu crouched on the ground with sweat flowing right down to his heels. Then Po said, 'The perfect man may gaze at the blue sky above, dive down into the Yellow Springs below, wander along the eight directions of the world, and yet his spirit and his being will show no signs of change. But you cower in abject trepidation and your eyes mist over. Were you to take aim now, how could you expect to hit the target?'

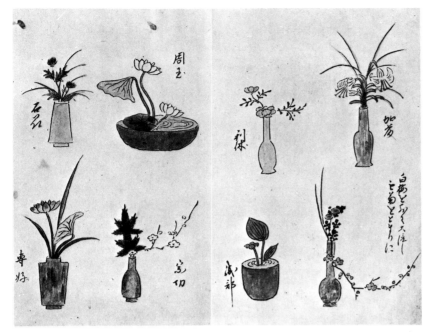

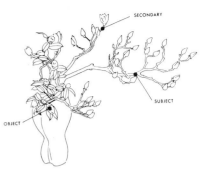

Related arts

This diagram helps the beginner to spot Heaven (subject), Man (second subject) and Earth (object). (From *The Masters' Book of Ikebana*, London and New York 1966, by courtesy of Bijutsu Shuppan-sha.)

Flower arrangements by early masters. Ikebana, the art of flower arrangement, became a Zen activity in Japan as early as the fourteenth century. Its basis is the relationship between Heaven, Man and Earth – all considered as states of mind. Thus, all flower arrangements have a tall central stem which represents Heaven, a medium-length stem for Man, and a short stem for Earth. Man is between Heaven and Earth, but the stems are not always arranged so that this is obvious. In the bottom left-hand corner the Heaven leaf can be seen soaring up to the right, the Man lotus flower rises next to it, and the Earth leaf turns downwards. But in the bottom right-hand corner the Heaven branch turns downwards, close to the ground, the Man leaf goes straight up, and the Earth flower ascends beside him. (Sketches of arrangements by early masters including Sen no Rikyo, two of his disciples, and Ikenobo Senko, from *Sansaiko Monjo*, ms. by Hosokawa Tadaoka Sansai, Japan, 16th–17th c. Misei Shigemori Collection, Tokyo.)

A Zen nun arranges branches. In this case Earth seems to have been allowed the same length as Heaven. (Photo by Nakada.)

In this jar of irises the Heaven leaf rises above the Man flower, while the Earth leaf curls down towards the earth. (A Jar of Irises, plate from *Soka Maragoromo* by Sounsai Chikuho, Japan, 1831. Ikenobo Junior College, Kyoto.)

Reverence in Zen means simplicity and the elimination of all that is unnecessary so that nothing stands in the way of the intuitive grasp of reality. In the making of tea and in serving it, all that is artificial is stripped away. Thus it is often used as an introduction to Zen for visitors at Zen monasteries. The atmosphere of the ceremony is gentle, light and harmonious, the teacups are handmade, a soft and restful light comes into the room, and the burning incense is also gentle and pervasive. The sound of the boiling water in the kettle is listened to peacefully, as all sense of hurry vanishes.
(An attendant dips the cup in water before the tea ceremony; tea room in Daitoku-ji Zen Monastery, Kyoto.)

The Japanese Noh drama has always been rooted in Zen. It is largely based on silence: the story is suggested rather than told. The end is achieved only through the ability of the actor, yet the protagonist's face is masked, and all the other actors are so economical in expression that Noh has been called 'frozen dancing'. This voiceless or 'inner' acting gives meaning to every movement, however trivial, and in fact even minute variations in interpretation give rise to different schools of acting. Yet there is no effect of rigidity in the play. Even to Western audiences, Noh conveys intense moments of sorrow, joy, bewilderment and other emotions, and the occasional tremendous shout of 'Hrruuhh!' can bring a spectator out of his seat. (Noh mask, Japan, 19th c. British Museum, London.)

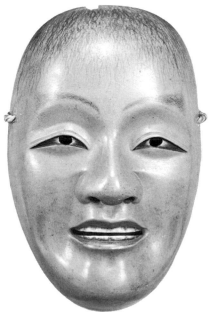

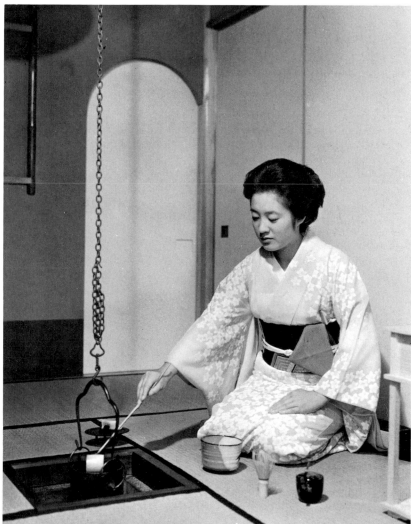

The Oxherding Sequence

The ox is probably the commonest domestic animal in China, and is certainly the most useful. This sequence of images, in which oxherding represents the Zen life, was first painted in the Sung period, by a pupil of Lin-chi (Rinzai), and thus its origin is early in Zen thought. In the first picture the boy oxherd searches for a lost ox (his own spiritual life, lost because he has been led astray by his deluded senses; it is typical of Chinese Ch'an/Zen thought to take such a practical animal to represent the spirit). Now he is rootless and homeless; but with the help of the Sutras (second picture) he begins to see traces of the ox despite his own confusion. In the third picture the boy's nature is opened through sound; he sees into the origin of things, and his senses settle into harmonious order. He sees the ox. In the fourth picture he almost has the ox, but because of pressures from the outside world, the ox is hard to control and struggles to return to its pleasant pasture. The boy has to be very hard on the ox. In the fifth picture the boy is just about controlling the ox, and in the sixth the struggle is over and he is on its back. He is no longer torn by the world of appearances, no longer concerned with gain and loss. He is indescribably joyful. In the seventh picture he recognizes the ox as a symbol and lets it go. He is now whole and serene. In the eighth both ox and man have vanished; the boy's mind is completely clear, and not even the concept of holiness remains. In picture nine the boy remains in immovable mind, seeing that waters are blue and mountains green, but not identifying himself with any change; 'Behold, the streams are flowing – whither nobody knows.' In the tenth and last picture he returns to the world, a free man, doing whatever he does with the whole of himself because there is nothing to gain. (The Ten Oxherding Pictures, paintings by Shu Sun after a set by Kakuan, Japan, 15th c. Shokoku-ji, Kyoto.)

Acknowledgments

The objects in the plates, pp. 33–64, are in the collections of Kansas City, William Rockhill Nelson Gallery of Art 49; London, British Library 41, 60, 61; London, British Museum 33, 36–37, 44, 48, 52, 56, 57, 59; London/San Francisco, Collection John Dugger Esq. 45; Private Collection 62, 63; Tokyo, Eisei Bunko 54; Tokyo, Idemitsu Art Gallery 35, 58; Tokyo, National Museum 47; Washington D.C., Freer Gallery of Art 43, 46; Collection Mrs Ayako Yoshikawa 38.

Photographs were supplied by Berlin, Staatliche Museen Preussischer Kulturbesitz 71 above l.; Robert S. Boni from Shunryu Suzuki, *Zen Mind, Beginner's Mind*, Weatherhill, New York 1970 69 below r.; Kyoto, Tankosha Publishing Company 90 below l. and r.; London, Camera Press 39, 42, 50, 51, 71 bottom, 73 above r. and below, 80, 81 above l. and r., centre, 82 r., 90 above, 91, 92 above r.; London, Japanese Information Centre 93 below r.; Hugh O'Donnell 64, 78, 79; Tokyo, Internat. Society for Educational Information 68 below; Tokyo, Sakamoto Photo Research Laboratory 38, 54, 63, 69 above l., 74 r., 75 above, 85 r., 88, 89 above, 93 above; Tokyo, Zauho Press 75 below, 85 l., 87 above l. and r.

Sources and further reading

Blyth, Reginald Horace, *Haiku*, Vols 1, 2, Tokyo 1960; *Zen in English Literature and Oriental Classics*, Tokyo 1942, New York 1960.

Chen-Chi, C., *The Practice of Zen*, London and New York 1960.

Cleary, Thomas and J. C. (trs.), *Blue Cliff Record*, Vols 1–3, Boulder 1977.

Conze, Edward, *Buddhist Scriptures*, Harmondsworth 1959.

Hakuin Zenji, *The Embossed Tea Kettle. Orate gama and other works of Hakuin Zenji*, London 1963.

Hanh, Tchich Nhat, *Zen Keys*, New York 1974.

Herrigel, Eugen, *The Method of Zen*, New York 1974, London 1976; *Zen in the Art of Archery*, New York 1953, London 1972.

Kapleau, Philip, *The Three Pillars of Zen*, New York 1966.

Leggett, Trevor, *Zen and the Ways*, Boulder 1977, London 1978.

Merton, Thomas, *Zen and the Birds of Appetite*, New York 1968.

Miura, Isshu, and Ruth Fuller Sasaki, *The Zen Koan*, New York 1965.

Reps, Saladin Paul (ed.), *Zen Flesh, Zen Bones. A Collection of Zen and pre-Zen Writing*, Tokyo and New York 1961, Harmondsworth 1971.

Robinson, G. W. (trs.), *Poems of Wang Wei*, Harmondsworth 1973.

Roshi, Kosho Uchiyama, *Approach to Zen*, Elmsford 1974.

Shibayama, Zenkei, *A Flower Does Not Talk*, Tokyo 1970; *Zen Comments on the Mumonkan*, New York 1975.

Sokei-an, Zen Master, of the First Zen Institute of America Inc., translator of the sayings of Hui Neng and the Record of Rinzai.

Suzuki, Daisetz Teitaro, *Essays in Zen Buddhism*, Series 1–3, London and New York 1949–53, in *The Complete Works of D. T. Suzuki*, London 1970; *Zen and Japanese Culture*, Princeton 1970.

Suzuki, Shunryu, *Zen Mind, Beginner's Mind*, New York 1970.

Watts, Alan, *The Spirit of Zen. A Way of Life, Work and Art in the Far East*, London 1959, New York 1960; *The Way of Zen*, New York 1957, Harmondsworth 1962.

Yokoi, Yuho and Daizen Victoria, *Zen Master Dogen. An Introduction with Selected Writings*, New York 1976.